SCANDINAVIAN INSTITUTE OF ASIAN STUDIES MONOGRAPH SERIES NO 14

Pali Buddhist Texts

Explained to the Beginner

Rune E A Johansson

LONDON AND NEW YORK

Scandinavian Institute of Asian Studies
Kejsergade 2, DK-1155 Copenhagen K.

First published 1973
Second edition, revised and enlarged 1977
Third edition, revised 1981

Published by Routledge
2 Park Square, Milton Park, Abingdon, Oxon, OX14 4RN
270 Madison Ave, New York NY 10016

Transferred to Digital Printing 2007

ISBN 0 7007 0063 3
ISSN 0069 1712

Sole distributors in India:
India Book House, Bombay and branches

Publisher's Note
The publisher has gone to great lengths to ensure the quality of this reprint but points out that some imperfections in the original may be apparent

PREFACE TO THE THIRD EDITION

To the second edition of this book an appendix was added, in which another major text, selected from Sutta Nipata, was introduced and explained. Some other additions and corrections were also given. In the preparation of this third edition the text has again been checked and a few more additions and corrections found desirable. They are given overleaf.

My thanks are renewed to The Scandinavian Institute of Asian Studies for its sponsorship of this book, and to Dr. Else Pauly, Dr. O.B. Anderson, Dr. J. Ergardt, my wife and others who have expressed their interest and offered their encouragement in the work.

1981 RJ

ADDENDA AND CORRIGENDA

P 19, line 10: *sattharaṃ*, should be *satthāraṃ*
P 19, line 13: *brahmaṇānaṃ*, should be *brāhmaṇānaṃ*
P 19, line 34: *satthugarava*, should be *satthugārava*
P 20, line 16 and P 21, line 29: *brahmaṇa*, should be *brāhmaṇa*
P 38, line 4: remove the comma after *katamā*.
P 40, line 16, P 44, line 19, and P 45, line 34: touch; add: lit "(object) to be touched", f p p to *phusati*, touch. G 7c
P 99, line 10 and P 126, line 17: *sabbaso* is called abl. It would be more exact to say that -*so* is an adverbial ending expressing measure.
P 110, line 7: The interpretation of *ubbandhaṃ* is doubtful. The feminine form of pres p nom sg is normally *ubbandhantī*. But at least of many verbs an abbreviated pres p in -*a* can also be found; a nom m *ubbandho* would be inflected like *sacca* and a form *ubbandhaṃ* could be acc m and f and nom and acc nt. Perhaps *ubbandhaṃ* in the text is meant as a nom nt sg adapted to *varaṃ*: "the (act of) hanging myself here is better than ..."
P 116, line 9: *sambuddha*; add: (cf *buddha*, p p of *bujjhati*, be awake, understand)
P 121, line 31: sg, should be pl, lit "they could tell", i e "one could describe"
P 126, line 18: The ablative case may also express the cause: *Kāmato jāyati soko*, "From love sorrow is born"
P 126, line 21: The locative case is also used in order to express sphere, circumstance, reference and similar relations: *Kankhā dhamme*, "doubt about the doctrine", *satipaṭṭhānesu supatiṭṭhitacitta*, "with a mind well based on the bases of mindfulness", *So seṭṭho deva-mānuse*, "he is the best among gods and men", *Brahmacariyaṃ Sugate caramase*, "may we live the chaste life with the Happy One"
P 127: two notes should be added:

1. In nt pl acc we sometimes find the ending -*e*. E g *rūpe* (No. 14 and 19), *phoṭṭhabbe* (No. 14)
2. In f sg instr, dat, gen, abl and loc the ending -*āya* can be replaced by -*ā*. E g instr *sikkhā* (No. 17)

P 147, line 26: *udyate*, should be *ucyate*
P 148, line 4: *sakkhīti*, should be *sakkhiti*.

CONTENTS

INTRODUCTION

Pali is known mainly as the language of Theravada Buddhism. The word Pāli[1] means "text", and the language is "the language of the texts". Very little is known about its origin. We do not know where it was spoken or if it originally was a spoken language at all. The ancient Ceylonese tradition says that the Buddha himself spoke Māgadhī and that this language was identical with Pali. The Buddha was born in Kapilavastu (perhaps 563 BC), a town in Nepal, and he spent most of his time in the kingdoms of Māgadha, Kośala, Vatsa and Vṛji, all of them close to Ganges. It is therefore quite probable that he spoke Māgadhī and perhaps other middle Indian dialects as well. We know, however, that Māgadhī, although a related dialect, differed from Pali in many respects, and the origins of Pali are now usually sought in other parts of North India. It is not known, whether the Buddhist doctrine ever was written down in Māgadhī. The art of writing was not used until centuries after the death of the Buddha. However this may be, we know for certain, that the Buddhist canonical literature has been preserved in Ceylon, written in the Pali language, and that this language for centuries remained the language used by the community of monks: commentaries and Buddhist treatises were written in Pali during centuries, and even a number of historical works. How and when the language came to Ceylon is not known: it must have been a north Indian language, and it may have been introduced into Ceylon in connection with some Buddhist missionary activity there. In fact, chronicles tell us that the famous king Asoka (about 274-234 BC) sent his son Mahinda on a mission of this type.

Pali was for a long time also used as a spoken language in the monasteries, and it is still possible to find monks in the Theravada countries who can speak it. One of these monks has even published a small textbook on this subject (Buddhadatta Mahathera, Aids to Pali Conversation and Translation).

The interest in the Pali language and literature has been steadily growing in the West during the last few decades, and the main part of the canonical literature has been published both in the original language and in translation. Behind this we find a growing concern with Buddhism: its dynamic

---

1) Pronounced with a long a, as in "father".

conception of man, its analysis of human psychology, its empirical and anti-metaphysical attitude, its tolerance, its demand for personal development - all this has made a deep impression on the Western mind. Jainism, another religion from the same time which also has produced an extensive literature written in a related dialect, has not attracted anything like this attention. To be sure, Pali literature gives expression only to the doctrines of one of the several Buddhist sects (Theravada, "the teaching of the elders"). Scriptures belonging to other sects, especially the many Mahayana sects, are known in other languages: Sanskrit, Tibetan, Chinese, Japanese, to mention only the most important. But there is reason to believe, that the Pali Buddhism best has preserved the original ideas, and as the least speculative and most "modern" in its general outlook it has aroused most interest (possibly with the exception of the Japanese Zen Buddhism).

The background of the present publication is this growing interest in Early Buddhism and its language. Its aim is to give an introduction into both at the same time. Fifty-two short extracts from the texts are quoted in Pali. They are so selected that they together will form a small compendium of the Buddhist doctrine. All of them are of central importance and well worth all the labour that the reader would care to devote to them. To every section, a complete vocabulary is given, explaining every word. Then comes a translation to normal English and a commentary which explains both linguistic difficulties and the content. After the texts, an abbreviated grammar is given, where the reader can find most of the forms met with in the texts.

Pali, like all classical languages, is mastered by reading the texts, not by speaking and imitating. Whatever is the main interest of the student, the language or Buddhism, the same texts will form his natural source of information. The best way of helping him will in both cases be to give him such explanations that he can read the texts directly, with only a minimum of preparation and difficulties. So the procedure recommended is this. Readers who are familiar with Sanskrit should start with the last chapter, "Pali and Sanskrit", which explains the relation between the two languages. Other readers should simply disregard this chapter and start by glancing through "Summary of Grammar" in order to get a general idea of the nature and pecularities of Pali. After a quick orientation in the Grammar, he can select any text that takes his fancy: he can, for instance, read the translations and then select a text which he likes or finds simple enough. Since every word has been translated and analyzed grammatically, he should be able to decipher the Pali text. Then he should read the text again and again until every word and construction has become meaningful to him.

To the majority of those mainly interested in Buddhism it would seem quite unnecessary to study the language. Are not all the important books translated to English? It is true that they are, and also that we can learn much about Buddhism without knowing Pali or any other of the main languages of Buddhism, just as we can learn much about Christianity without learning Hebrew and Greek. But there are special difficulties in Buddhism. Even very popular books about Buddhism commonly make use of quite a few Pali words, at least kamma and nibbana which cannot be translated, but usually many more. There is an extensive technical terminology in Buddhism, which can be explained but not properly translated. In many cases we find different opinions about the correct interpretation of a term or a doctrine, and in the popular books about Buddhism much is misleading or controversial. The only way to overcome these difficulties and reach a real understanding is therefore to be able to read the most important texts in the original language and judge for oneself. An elementary knowledge of Pali is therefore no luxury. In the present state of affairs, it is simply the only way. Our purpose is to help the reader take the first steps towards this goal.

Pali is an Indo-European language, closely related to Sanskrit, the most important literary language of ancient India, and ultimately also related to most European languages. Its similarities to English are not very striking but may perhaps be guessed from parallels like me "by me", sūpa "soup", bhātar "brother", nava "new", vamati "vomit". It has a rich inflectional system. The noun and the adjective has, just as in its mother language, Sanskrit, eight different cases, although some of them have lost their separate forms. By means of the case forms, relations are expressed which we usually render by means of prepositions, e g tassa "to him" (dative) or "his" (genitive), agginā "by means of fire" (instrumental), tasmiṃ samaye "at this time" (locative). The verb has special terminations for the different persons, e g asmi "I am", atthi "he is". There is a present tense, a future tense and a past tense, called aorist. They are formed through modifications of the stem. Cf

karomi "I do" (present tense)
karissāmi "I shall do" (future tense)
akaraṃ "I did" (aorist)

It will be found that -iss- is the characteristic of the future tense, and the so-called augment a- is one of the elements that we usually find in the past tense. More difficult to cope with are the frequent compounds and absolute expressions which are used to express subordinate facts and circumstances: disvā "having seen"; gate, ṭhite etc (text No. 36) "whether he goes, stands etc", lit. "in (him) being gone, put upright" (locative); dukkha - nirodha- gāminī-paṭipadā (text No. 5) "the way going to the cessation of suffering". Constructions of these types sometimes require careful analysis in order to be understood correctly.

There are several types of literature written in Pali. Oldest and most important is the Buddhist canonical literature (Tipiṭaka). Among the later works we find extensive commentaries, historical works and independent treatises on religious subjects.

The canonical literature is divided into three great collections, called piṭaka "baskets". Vinaya-piṭaka is mainly an exposition of the rules valid for monks and nuns. Sutta-piṭaka is more extensive and more varied. Four parts, called Nikāya (collection) describe the life and activities of the Buddha. Certain episodes from his life are told, and a great number of his discussions with disciples and laymen are reported. Even teaching given by his most important disciples can be found in the Nikāyas. A fifth collection contains a number of very heterogeneous works: the great collection of birth stories (Jātaka), the poetic compilations Dhammapada, Theragāthā, Therīgāthā, Sutta Nipāta, and a number of others. The third basket, Abhidhamma-piṭaka, is more voluminous than the two others and is certainly of later origin. It consists of philosophical treatises, sometimes of an abstruse character, and is so far incompletely understood.

When reading the early Buddhist literature we must not forget how these works originated. The Buddha himself and his disciples could not write. It was an old tradition in Indian cultural life that compositions in prose as well as poetry should be learned literally by heart, and they were in this way transferred from generation to generation. Matter that is conserved in this way will necessarily get a special character. We must expect less homogeneity than we are used to nowadays: a work will never get a fixed and definite form, there will be misunderstandings, gaps and additions. Repetitions, stereotype phrases and formulas will be common. Just like this is the Buddhist prose. The poetry often consists of compressed doctrinal formulas, composed mainly as an aid to memory. We often find it difficult to appreciate this literature, especially in translation. But, on the other hand, it is not difficult to find passages, both in prose and poetry, of great beauty and force. There are formulations that feel fresh and reveal the deep psychological understanding of their originator. We feel behind them the seriousness and enthusiasm of the first Buddhists, and we even can glimpse something of the tremendousness of the great experience, which was then the goal of the doctrine.

The texts quoted in this book are selected from the following works, all of them forming parts of the Sutta Piṭaka[1]:

Dīgha Nikāya, "Dialogues of the Buddha"
Majjhima Nikāya, "Middle Length Sayings"
Samyutta Nikāya, "Kindred Sayings"
Anguttara Nikāya, "Gradual Sayings"
Sutta Nipāta, "Woven Cadences"
Dhammapada, "The Way of the Doctrine"

1) except one passage which has been selected from the much later work Visuddhimagga, "The Path of Purity", by Buddhaghosa.

Udāna, "Verses of Uplift"
Theragāthā, "Psalms of the Brethren"
Therīgāthā, "Psalms of the Sisters"

The texts have been quoted from the editions of the Pali Text Society, London. The English titles given above are the titles of the English translations of these works, also published by the Pali Text Society. The only exception is Dhammapada which has been quoted from the text edited by S. Radhakrishnan (Oxford Univ. Press, London 1950).

PRONUNCIATION

Pali has been written in several different alphabets. In European editions of the texts, the Roman script has been used consistently. The systems of transcription have varied to some extent. Here follows an account of the letters used in this book and the sounds they represent.

a, i, u are short vowels, like in "hut", "bit", "put".
ā, ī, ū are long, pure vowels, like in "father", "tree", "cool".
e is a pure, long sound, like in "bed", but long.
If followed by two consonants it should be pronounced short.
o is a pure, long sound, like o in "more".
Before two consonants, it is the same sound but short.
ṃ is a sign of nasalization: the vowel preceding ṃ should be pronounced through the nose.
k like k in "skate" or c in "cool".
g like g in "grey".
j like j in "just".
t like t in "till" (a rather hard t, without aspiration, like in French).
d like d in "dull".
n like n in "no", but before g and k like n in "pink", "finger".
p like p in "push".
b like b in "bake".
m like m in "me".
r like r in "rich".
l and ḷ like l in "long".
y like y in "yes".
v like v in "vowel". Some pronounce it like English w, either in all positions or only when it is combined with another consonant.
s like s in "sign".
kh, gh, jh, th, dh, ph, bh are pronounced like k, g, j, t, d, p and b but with a strong aspiration. Pronounce like hot-house, buck-horn, dog-house, hard-hearted, etc.
c like ch in "child".
ch is an aspirated c, like church-hall.
ñ like Spanish ñ in "mañana" or like English ny in "canyon".
ṭ, ṭh, ḍ, ḍh, ṇ are called cerebral or retroflex sounds because they should be pronounced with the tip of the tongue bent slightly upwards and backwards. A tendency in this direction is naturally produced

by English speakers when pronouncing combinations like tr in "try", rt in "heart", and dr in "dry" (but t and d should be hard sounds, not as soft as tr and dr in "try" and "dry").

h is said to have been a voiced sound. Since we do not know exactly how it was done, we pronounce it like the English h.

Every sound should be properly spoken and not swallowed or blurred. Long and short syllables must be kept apart, which means that long vowels must be spoken long and double consonants must be spoken double.

How the Pali words were stressed at the time when the oldest texts were written is not known. There are however indications that the musical Vedic accents were no longer used but that rather a system depending on the quantity of the syllables was followed. From certain phonetical developments it seems probable that a stress accent following about the same rules as those valid for Classical Sanskrit was used at the times of Early Buddhism. According to these rules, the second syllable from the end should be stressed if it is long or if the word has only two syllables: bhū´ta, sac´ca, ha´ta, upanī´ta, paccat´taṃ. If this syllable is short, the third from the end should be stressed, if it is long, otherwise the fourth from the end: anā´laya, ka´tama, paccāgac´chati, ve´diyati, bhā´vana, nijigiṃ´sanatā. A syllable is long either because it has a long vowel or because it has a short vowel followed by two consonants (th, bh etc are counted as one consonant). However, in Pali as it is spoken now, stress seems to be without importance. The quantity of syllables is carefully observed but the stress is fairly even.

SANDHI

Linguistic sounds are frequently modified when immediately followed or preceded by certain other sounds. In English, for instance, the *sc-* in "science" is not the same sound as the *-sc-* in "conscience", and the *-s* in "goes into" is not identical with the *-s* in "goes to". These phonetic changes may be more or less subtle, and in European languages they are usually not recorded in writing, neither within nor between words. But in ancient India it was the tradition to record them faithfully. In consequence, the beginning and ending of words are sometimes written in a way that makes the words difficult to recognize: these changes are called *sandhi* (junction). The most common types of sandhi are recorded below (the sign > means: "has changed into").

1. Two similar vowels may fuse into one long vowel: *a* + *a* = *ā* (*na asātaṃ* > *nāsātaṃ*, No. 10), *ā* + *a* = *ā* (*avijjā-anusaya* > *avijjānusaya*, No. 10).

2. If two vowels meet, the first one may be elided: *pana assa* > *pan'assa* (No. 36), *pi icchaṃ* > *p'icchaṃ* (No. 2), *ti eva* > *t'eva* (No. 14), *tena eva* > *ten'eva* (No. 14), *ca evaṃ* > *c'evaṃ* (No. 14). Even *-aṃ* may be elided: *taṃ ahaṃ* > *tāhaṃ* (No. 26). The second vowel may be lengthened: *seyyathā idaṃ* > *seyyathīdaṃ* (No. 3), *satta upalabbhati* > *sattūpalabbhati* (No. 8). But it may also remain short: *pañca upādāna* > *pañcupādāna* (No. 2). Elisions are in some editions marked by an apostrophe, in others not.

3. Before *ti* and *pi*, any short vowel may be lengthened (they were originally *iti* and *api*): *hoti ti* > *hotī ti* (No. 15), *uppajjatu ti* > *uppajjatū ti* (No. 18).

4. If two vowels meet, the second one may be elided, and the first may be lengthened: *tayo ime* > *tayo me* (No. 12), *ṭhito amhi iti* > *ṭhito'mhīti* (No. 36), *cāri ahaṃ* > *cāri'haṃ* (No. 46).

5. A consonant may be inserted between two vowels: *na idha* > *na-y-idha* (No. 8), *adukkha asukhā* > *adukkha-m-asukhā* (No. 10), *cha imā* > *cha-y-imā*, *eva* > *yeva* (No. 38); *sammā aññā* > *sammadaññā*, *tasmā iha* > *tasmātiha*, *yathā iva* > *yathariva*.

6. A final consonant may be adapted phonetically to the initial consonant of the next word: katamaṃ ca > katamañ ca (No. 2), viññāṇaṃ ti eva > viññāṇan-t'eva (No. 14), yaṃ nūna ahaṃ > yannūnāhaṃ (No. 26), hadayaṃ-gama > hadayan-gama (No. 30), taṃ pi > tam pi (No. 2). A final ṃ may be changed to m before a vowel: evaṃ āha > evam āha (No. 1).

7. After a final vowel, an initial consonant may be doubled: paṭhama-jhānaṃ > paṭhamajjhānaṃ (No. 38), dukkha-khandhassa > dukkhakkhandhassa (No. 19), upādāna-khandha > upādānakkhandha (No. 2), pamāda-ṭhāna > pamādaṭṭhāna (No. 32).

8. Sometimes both sounds are changed: yaṃ yad > yañ ñad (No. 14), tvaṃ eva > tvañ ñeva.

LIST OF ABBREVIATIONS

abl	ablative
acc	accusative
act	active
adj	adjective
adv	adverb
aor	aorist
cond	conditional tense
dat	dative
dem	demonstrative
f	feminine
f p p	future passive participle
fut	future tense
G	Summary of Grammar
gen	genitive
ger	gerund
imper	imperative
ind	indicative
inf	infinitive
instr	instrumental
lit	literally
loc	locative
m	masculine
med	medium conjugation
No	Text number
nt	neuter
nom	nominative
opt	optative
P	Pali
part	participle
pass	passive
perf	perfect tense
pl	plural
p p	past participle
pres	present tense
pres p	present participle
pron	pronoun
rel	relative
sg	singular
S	Sanskrit
voc	vocative

CONTENT ANALYSIS OF THE TEXTS

1. EXPERIENCE IS THE ONLY CRITERION (Majjhima Nikaya I 265)

- Api nu tumhe bhikkhave evaṃ jānantā evaṃ passantā evaṃ vadeyyātha: Satthā no garu, satthugāravena ca mayaṃ vademāti.
- No h'etaṃ bhante.
- Api nu tumhe bhikkhave evaṃ jānantā evaṃ passantā evaṃ vadeyyātha: Samaṇo no evam-āha samaṇā ca, na ca mayaṃ evaṃ vademāti.
- No h'etaṃ bhante.
- Api nu tumhe bhikkhave evaṃ jānantā evaṃ passantā aññaṃ sattharaṃ uddiseyyāthāti.
- No h'etaṃ bhante.
- Api nu tumhe bhikkhave evaṃ jānantā evaṃ passantā yāni tāni puthu-samaṇa-brahmaṇānaṃ vata-kotūhala-mangalāni tāni sārato paccāgaccheyyāthāti.
- No h'etaṃ bhante.
- Nanu bhikkhave yad-eva tumhākaṃ sāmaṃ ñātaṃ sāmaṃ diṭṭhaṃ sāmaṃ viditaṃ tad-eva tumhe vadethāti.
- Evaṃ bhante.
- Sādhu bhikkhave. Upanītā kho me tumhe bhikkhave iminā sandiṭṭhikena dhammena akālikena ehipassikena opanayikena paccattaṃ veditabbena viññūhi.

api + opt,	"perhaps", indicates a question	
nu	an interrogative particle reinforcing other interrogative words or indicating a question	
tumhe	you (nom pl to tvaṃ you)[x]	
bhikkhu	m monk (voc pl)	[S bhikṣu]
evaṃ	so	
jānāti	know (pres p nom pl)	[S √jñā]
passati	see (pres p nom pl)	[S √paś]
vadati	speak (opt 2 pl, G6c)	[S √vad]
satthar	m teacher	
no	enclitic gen to mayaṃ we	(G 4a)
garu	heavy, venerated	[S guru]
gārava	m respect; satthugarava respect for the teacher (instr sg)	
ca	and	

[x] The form occurring in the text is explained within brackets after the translation.

vadeti	speak (pres 1 pl; vademāti = vadema ti)	
ti	marks end of quotation	
no	indeed not (na+u)	[S na "not", u "also"]
hi	because, surely	
etaṃ	that (nt nom sg)	
bhante	sir (voc of polite address)	
samaṇa	m recluse, wanderer (nom sg, and then nom pl)	[S śramaṇa]
no	enclitic dat to mayaṃ we	(G 4a)
āha	perf (he) spoke	(G 6g)
na	not	
añña	another	[S anya]
uddisati	appoint (opt 2 pl)	[S √diś]
yāni tāni	(rel pron + dem pron nt pl) those which	(G 4c, e)
puthu	various, ordinary	[S pṛthu]
brahmaṇa	m brahmin (gen pl)	
vata	m, nt rite, observance	[S vrata]
kotūhala	nt festival	
mangala	nt good omen, ceremony	
sāra	m essence	
paccāgacchati	fall back on, return to (opt 2 pl)	[S prati-ā-√ gam]
nanu	interrogative particle, "is it not?"	
yad	rel pron sg nt, which	
eva	only, just	
tvaṃ	you (tumhākaṃ gen or dat pl)	(G 4b)
sāmaṃ	self, of oneself	
ñāta	p p known (jānāti know)	[S √jñā]
diṭṭha	p p seen (dassati see)	[S √dṛś]
vidita	p p found (vindati find)	[S √vid]
sādhu	good	
upanīta	brought up (p p nom pl m of upaneti bring up)	[S √nī]
kho	indeed	
me	by me (enclitic instr to ahaṃ I)	
ayaṃ	this (iminā instr sg m)	(G 4d)
sandiṭṭhika	visible (instr sg)	[S √dṛś]
dhamma	m doctrine	[S dharma]
akālika	immediate, timeless	
ehipassika	verifiable	[S √i √paś]
opanayika	leading to (the goal), effective	[S √nī]
paccattaṃ	adv individually	
veditabba	f p p to be known (vedeti know)	[S √vid]
viññū	intelligent, wise (instr pl)	

"Monks, would you perhaps, when you know and see this, speak so: 'Our teacher is venerable and we speak out of respect for our teacher'?"

"Certainly not, sir!"

"Monks, would you perhaps, when you know and see this, speak so: 'A recluse spoke so to us, and (or) recluses, but we do not speak so'?"

"Certainly not, sir!"

"Monks, would you perhaps, when you know and see this, look out for another teacher?"

"Certainly not, sir!"

"Monks, would you perhaps, when you know and see this, return to the observances, festivals and ceremonies of the ordinary recluses and Brahmins, considering these to be the essence?"

"Certainly not, sir!"

"Monks, do you not speak that which is known by yourselves, seen by yourselves, found by yourselves?"

"Yes, sir!"

"Good, monks! You, monks, have been instructed by me through this timeless doctrine which can be realized and verified, leads to the goal, and can be understood individually by the intelligent."

Notes

"when you know and see this": the doctrine of dependent origination has just been discussed; cf text No. 19.

vadeyyātha: the optative tense is used for hypothetical actions: "would you say?"

A samaṇa was an itinerant philosopher or preacher: samaṇo .... samaṇā ca probably means "one or more recluses".

brahmaṇa "Brahmin", i e member of the Indian priest caste. The word is used in this sense here, but in Buddhist texts it may also refer to any person of high moral stature or a person who has attained the Buddhist ideal.

sārato: -to is a suffix with ablative meaning, lit "from the essence": it is often used in comparisons, therefore "as the essence", "as the main thing".

yāni tāni refers to -mangalāni; this combination of a rel pron and dem pron is commonly used to anticipate and emphasize something; we would say "just these".

sāmaṃ: indeclinable pron "by oneself"; tumhākaṃ is probably gen to this, "by yourselves".

ehipassika: an adj constructed by adding the adjective suffix -ika to two imperatives: ehi "come!" passa "see!" lit "come-and-see-ish", "to be directly experienced".

2. DEFINITION OF SUFFERING (Digha Nikaya II 305)

Katamañ ca, bhikkhave, dukkhaṃ ariya-saccaṃ?

Jāti pi dukkhā, jarā pi dukkhā, maraṇam pi dukkham, soka-parideva--dukkha-domanass-upāyāsā pi dukkhā, yam p'icchaṃ na labhati tam pi dukkhaṃ, sankhittena pañcupādānakkhandhā dukkhā.

katama	which? (nom sg nt, aṃ > añ before c)	
ca	and (always placed after the first word of a clause or phrase)	
bhikkhu	m monk (voc pl)	
dukkha	adj painful; nt suffering	[S duḥkha]
ariya	noble	[S ārya]
sacca	adj true; nt truth (G 8c)	[S satya]
jāti	f birth	
pi	also, even	
jarā	f old age	
maraṇa	nt death	
soka	m grief, sorrow	[S śoka]
parideva	m lamentation	
domanassa	nt depression, unhappiness	
upāyāsa	m misery, despair (nom pl, because the compounded nouns are coordinated; taken together they form plural)	
yaṃ ··· taṃ	that which .... that	
p' = pi		
icchati	wish (pres p nom sg m "wishing")	[S √iṣ]
na	not	
labhati	get, obtain	[S √labh]
sankhitta	concise (instr sg "briefly")	[S √kṣip]
pañca	five	
upādāna	nt attachment, dependence, basis	
khandha	m group, factor (nom pl)	[S skandha]

Monks, what is the noble truth about suffering?

Birth is suffering, old age is suffering, death is suffering, grief, lamentation, discomfort, unhappiness and despair are suffering; to wish for something and not obtain it is suffering; briefly, the five factors of attachment are suffering.

Notes

In the first sentence there is no finite verb: the copula hoti or atthi "is" is usually omitted.

In texts No. 2-5 the four basic truths are defined. Their names are dukkhaṃ ariya-saccaṃ (No. 2), dukkha-samudayaṃ ariya-saccaṃ (No. 3), dukkha-nirodhaṃ ariya-saccaṃ (No. 4), dukkha-nirodha-gāminī-paṭipadā ariya-saccaṃ (No. 5). Syntactically, these expressions are somewhat loosely formulated and of different types. Note that samudaya and nirodha are masculine and therefore must be acc sg, if the compounds are not of the possessive type and therefore adjectively adapted to saccaṃ; paṭipadā can only be nom sg. In English we find expressions that are nearly as loose. We cannot speak about "pain truth", but we say "tea-bag" and "nerve cell". Probably dukkhaṃ and paṭipadā should be understood as nom and be translated "truth (which is) pain" = "truth about pain"; dukkha-samudayaṃ and dukkha-nirodhaṃ are probably possessive compounds (G 8f) adjectively related to saccaṃ and therefore nom sg nt, lit "pain-originating truth", "pain-ceasing truth", i e "truth about the origin of pain", "truth about the cessation of pain". There are other possibilities: dukkhaṃ (No. 2) may also be adj and so the same type of attribute as dukkha-samudayaṃ taken as poss compound; it may also be taken as acc sg of the noun, because acc is sometimes used as a "case of reference", although the loc is more common in this function; dukkha-samudayaṃ and dukkha-nirodhaṃ could also be understood as acc of reference. On the other hand, paṭipadā (No. 5) is certainly nom, if it should not simply be combined with ariya-saccaṃ to form one long compound. Dukkha is a very common word in Buddhism. It is usually translated by "suffering" and we shall keep that but remember that the real meaning is somewhat more vague and general, something like "discomfort", "unhappiness", "unpleasantness", "frustration".

Jāti pi dukkhā: note that dukkhā is treated as an adj and given the feminine termination since jāti is fem .

yam p'icchaṃ etc, lit: "what one, although wishing, not gets, that is suffering".

yam is rel pron and object to icchaṃ.

upādānakkhandhā, either "the basic factors" or "the factors (leading to) attachment"; they are rūpa "form", "body"; vedanā "feeling", saññā "ideation", sankhāra "activity", "energy" and viññāṇa "consciousness". These factors are an instrument of our attachment to the world and a basis of rebirth. Suffering is therefore a basic function of our psycho-physical constitution.

3. THE CAUSE OF SUFFERING (Digha Nikaya II 308)

Katamañ ca, bhikkhave, dukkha-samudayaṃ ariya-saccaṃ?
Yāyaṃ taṇhā ponobhavikā nandi-rāga-sahagatā tatra tatrābhinandinī, seyyathīdaṃ kāma-taṇhā bhava-taṇhā vibhava-taṇhā.

katama	which?	
ca	and	
bhikkhu	m monk (voc pl)	
dukkha	adj painful; nt suffering	
samudaya	m origin	[S sam - ud√i]
ariya	noble	
sacca	adj true; nt truth	
ya	which (here yā rel pron fem nom sg) (G 4e)	
ayaṃ	this; yā ayaṃ just this (G 4d)	
taṇhā	f thirst, craving	[S tṛṣṇā]
ponobhavika	leading to rebirth	
nandi	f pleasure	
rāga	m emotion, passion	
sahagata	"gone together with", connected with	[S√gam]
tatra tatra	here and there	
abhinandin	finding pleasure in (fem nom sg)	
seyyathā	such as	
idaṃ	this (G 4d)	
seyyathīdaṃ	i e, namely	
kāma	m love, pleasure	
bhava	m becoming, rebirth	[S√bhu]
vibhava	m annihilation	

Monks, what is the noble truth about the origin of suffering?
Just this craving, leading to rebirth, accompanied by pleasure and emotion, and finding satisfaction now here now there, namely the craving for sense-pleasure, the craving for new life and the craving for annihilation.

Note

The rel pron ya is sometimes used in combination with a dem pron to introduce definitions and general statements. It has then a deictic or emphatic function, "just this".

4. THE CESSATION OF SUFFERING (Digha Nikaya II 310)

Katamañ ca, bhikkhave, dukkha-nirodhaṃ ariya-saccaṃ?
Yo tassā yeva taṇhāya asesa-virāga-nirodho cāgo paṭinissaggo mutti anālayo.

katama	which?
ca	and
bhikkhu	m monk (voc pl)
dukkha	adj painful; nt suffering
nirodha	m cessation (here with neuter ending because adapted, as possessive compound, to saccaṃ) [S √rudh suppress]
ariya	noble
sacca	nt truth
ya	rel pron (yo nom sg m) (G 4e)
so, ta	he, that (tassā gen fem sg) (G 4c)
(y)eva	just, certainly
taṇhā	f thirst, craving (gen sg)
asesa	without remainder, complete
virāga	m freedom from desire, indifference (towards)
cāga	m abandoning [S tyāga]
paṭinissagga	m rejecting, renouncing [S prati-nis-√sṛj]
mutti	f release, freedom [S mukti]
anālaya	m aversion

Monks, what is the noble truth about the cessation of suffering?
Just the complete indifference to and cessation of that very craving, the abandoning of it, the rejection of it, the freedom from it, the aversion towards it.

Note

Yo is rel pron but, just as in text No. 2, the clause is not relative. It agrees with nirodho and has a deictic function: "just this".

5. THE WAY TO FREEDOM FROM SUFFERING (Dīgha Nikaya II 311)

Katamañ ca, bhikkhave, dukkha-nirodha-gāminī-paṭipadā ariya-saccaṃ?

Ayam eva ariyo aṭṭhangiko maggo, seyyathīdaṃ samma-diṭṭhi sammā-sankappo sammā-vācā sammā-kammanto sammā-ājīvo sammā-vāyāmo sammā-sati sammā-samādhi.

katama	which?	
ca	and	
bhikkhu	m monk (voc pl)	
dukkha	nt suffering	
nirodha	m cessation	
gāmin	going (nom f sg)	
paṭipadā	f way	
ariya	noble	
sacca	nt truth	
ayaṃ	this	
eva	just, exactly	
aṭṭhangika	having eight (aṭṭha) limbs or parts (anga)	
magga	m way	
seyyathā	such as	
idaṃ	nt this	
seyyathīdaṃ	i e, namely	
sammā	rightly, perfectly	[S samyak]
diṭṭhi	f view, opinion	[S dṛṣṭi]
sankappa	m intention, purpose	[S saṃkalpa]
vācā	f speech	
kammanta	m action, work, behaviour	
ājīva	m livelihood	
vāyāma	m effort	
sati	f mindfulness	[S smṛti]
samādhi	m concentration	

Monks, what is the noble truth about the way that goes to the cessation of suffering?

Just this noble eightfold way, namely right view, right purpose, right speech, right action, right livelihood, right effort, right mindfulness, and right concentration.

Note

A more detailed presentation of the eight parts of the way will be found in texts No. 27–44.

samma-diṭṭhi etc, note that an adverb like sammā can be joined to a noun to form a compound, where we must use an adjective in translation (G 8d).

6. THE IMPERMANENCE OF LIFE (Samyutta Nikaya I 109)

Accayanti ahorattā,
jīvitam uparujjhati,
āyu khīyati maccānam,
kunnadīnam va odakaṃ.

acceti or accayati	pass, elapse (3 pl pres)	[S ati-√i]
aho	nt day	
ratta	nt night	[S rātra]
ahorattā	days and nights	
jīvita	nt life	
uparujjhati	is stopped, annihilated (pass of uparundhati break up)	
āyu	nt life	
khīyati	is exhausted (pass of khayati)	
macca	m mortal (gen pl)	[S martya]
kunnadī	f small river (gen pl)	
va	like	
odaka	nt water	[S udaka]

Days and nights pass,
life runs to an end,
the life-span of mortals peters out
like the water of rivers.

7. THERE IS NO SOUL (Buddhaghosa, Visuddhimagga XVI 90)

Dukkham eva hi, na koci dukkhito,
kārako na, kiriyā va vijjati,
atthi nibbuti, na nibbuto pumā,
maggam atthi, gamako na vijjati.

dukkha	nt suffering	
eva	just, certainly	
hi	for, namely	
na koci	nobody	
dukkhita	adj suffering	
kāraka	m one who does	[S √kṛ]
na	not	
kiriyā	f action, deed	
va = eva	even, certainly	
vijjati	is found (pass of vindati find)	
atthi	is	[S asti]
nibbuti	f cooling, peace, nirvana	
na ... pumā	nobody	
nibbuta	adj extinguished, appeased, having attained nirvana	
magga	m, here nt way	[S mārga]
gamaka	m walker	

For suffering is but no sufferer,
not the doer but certainly the deed is found,
peace is but not the appeased one,
the way is but the walker is not found.

Notes

Dukkham eva hi, add vijjati "is found" or "atthi" there is.
This verse is a famous and pointed formulation of the anatta doctrine. It should be noted that it denies the existence of an immortal soul rather than the unity and continuity of personality (see text No. 8 about

this). According to Buddhism there is no soul (*attā*) but certainly a coordinating center called mind (*citta*) by which the functional unity of human personality is effected. This internal center can be purified and developed and may attain nirvana (see text No. 46). But in the final analysis, the whole of personality is found to be made up of processes.

8. DEFINITION OF PERSONALITY (Samyutta Nikaya I 135)

The nun Vajirā was harrassed with doubts by Māra, the Tempter or god of Death: What is a "person"? How does he arise? Who creates him? However, Vajirā understood that questions of this type are misleading and gave the following answer:

Kinnu satto ti paccesi?
Māra, diṭṭhigataṃ nu te.
Suddha-sankhāra-puñjo yaṃ,
na-y-idha sattūpalabbhati.
Yathā hi angasambhārā
hoti saddo ratho iti,
evaṃ khandhesu santesu
hoti satto ti sammuti.

kin = kiṃ	what? why?	
nu	then, now	
satta	m being, person, essence, soul (from as be, pres p sant being)	
(i)ti	so (used to mark the end of a quotation)	
pacceti	come back to, fall back on (2 sg pres ind)	[S prati -√i]
diṭṭhi	f view, false theory	[S dṛṣṭi]
gata	gone (p p to gacchati go)	
tvaṃ	you (enclitic instr: te)	
suddha	pure, only	[S śuddha]
sankhāra	m activity, process	[S saṃskāra]
pũnja	m heap, mass	
yaṃ = ayaṃ	this	
na	not	
(y)idha	here	
upalabbhati	is found (pres ind pass to upalabhati get, find)	
yathā	as, like	
hi	for	
anga	nt limb, part	
sambhāra	m combination (abl sg)	
hoti = bhavati	becomes, is	
sadda	m sound, word	[S śabda]
ratha	m a two-wheeled carriage	

evaṃ	so	
khandha	m group, factor (loc pl)	[S skandha]
sant	being (loc pl, pres p)	
sammuti	f consent, general opinion, common parlance	

Why do you then harp on the word 'person'? Māra, you are starting from wrong premises. This is nothing but a lot of processes; no 'person' is found here. For just as the word 'carriage' is used when the parts are combined, so the word 'person' is commonly used when the factors are present.

Notes

diṭṭhigataṃ te, "by you is gone to false opinion", i e "you have got stuck in a wrong attitude".

sattūpalabbhati = satto upalabbhati "an essence is found".

anga-sambhārā abl sg "after combination of parts".

khandhesu santesu: an absolute locative corresponding to a temporal clause: "There being factors" = "when there are factors".

This text gives an uncommonly clear explanation of what the Buddhist anatta-doctrine really means. The usual word for "ego" or "soul" (attā) is not mentioned here, but we see from the context that satta is used in the same meaning. It is not the functional unity and continuity that is denied but only the "soul", i e a permanent and unchanging personality core. Just as a car has some sort of personality, defined as a "characteristic unity of parts", so has also the human being an empiric, functional personality, built up from factors (khandha). Modern Western psychology describes personality in terms that are not much different in principle.

9. THE FACTORS OF PERSONALITY (Majjhima Nikaya I 435)

So yad-eva tattha hoti rūpagataṃ vedanāgataṃ saññāgataṃ sankhāra-gataṃ viññāṇagataṃ te dhamme aniccato dukkhato rogato gaṇḍato sallato aghato ābādhato parato palokato suññato anattato samanupassati. So tehi dhammehi cittaṃ paṭivāpeti.

so	he, that	
yad	rel pron nt what (G 4e)	
eva	just, exactly	
tattha	there	
hoti = bhavati	is, becomes	
rūpa	nt form, matter, body	
gata	gone (p p to gacchati go), here: connected with, concerning	
vedanā	f feeling	
saññā	f perception, ideation, imaging	
sankhāra	m activity, energy, behaviour	
viññāṇa	nt consciousness	[S vijñāna]
te	they, those (nom pl to so he)	
dhamma	m thing	
anicca	impermanent (abl sg)	[S anitya]
dukkha	nt suffering	
roga	nt illness	
gaṇḍa	m swelling, boil	
salla	nt arrow	[S śalya]
agha	nt evil, pain	
ābādha	m disease, affliction	
para	other, strange	
paloka	m decay	
suñña	empty	[S śūnya]
anatta	without ego, without soul	[S an-ātman]
samanupassati	regard	
citta	nt mind	
paṭivāpeti	turn away from	

What there is with regard to form, feeling, ideas, activity and consciousness, he regards those things as impermanent, as suffering, as illness, as a boil, as an arrow, as evil, as an affliction, as alien, as empty, as soulless. He turns his mind away from those things.

Notes

"He" in the text refers to a meditating monk who analyzes himself as consisting of the five mentioned factors, all of them impermanent, impersonal and unpleasant. The text continues to describe how he turns his attention from these things toward something better: nirvana.

Dhamma is a word with complex meanings. It corresponds to S dharma, derived from dhṛ, "hold", "support". The original meaning therefore seems to have been "something substantial". In Buddhist writings it has come to extensive use within three areas:

a) objective meanings: thing, nature, rule (see texts No. 18,36, 47)

b) psychological meanings: idea, mental image, psychological state or process (the psychological contents observed by mano "the inner sense", see text No. 9, 11, 13, 14, 35, 52)

c) religious meaning: teaching, doctrine, especially the Buddhist doctrine (see text No. 1).

aniccato .... samanupassati: the ablative suffix -to may mean "with reference to", "in terms of" and so "as" in combination with "regard": "he regards as impermanent ..."

tehi dhammehi abl pl "from those things".

10. FEELING (Majjhima Nikaya I 302 f)

Tisso kho imā vedanā: sukhā vedanā, dukkhā vedanā, adukkha-m-asukhā vedanā ti.

Katamā pana sukhā vedanā, katamā dukkhā vedanā, katamā, adukkha-m-asukhā vedanā ti?

Yaṃ kho kāyikaṃ vā cetasikaṃ vā sukhaṃ sātaṃ vedayitaṃ ayaṃ sukhā vedanā. Yaṃ kho kāyikaṃ vā cetasikaṃ vā dukkhaṃ asātaṃ vedayitaṃ, ayaṃ dukkhā vedanā. Yaṃ kho kāyikaṃ vā cetasikaṃ vā n'eva sātaṃ nāsātaṃ vedayitaṃ, ayaṃ adukkha-m-asukhā vedanā ti .... Sukhāya kho vedanāya rāgānusayo pahātabbo, dukkhāya vedanāya paṭighānusayo pahātabbo, adukkha-m-asukhāya vedanāya avijjānusayo pahātabbo ti.

ti	three (m tayo, nt tiṇi, f tisso)	
kho	indeed	
ayaṃ	this (imā f nom pl)	
vedanā	f feeling (nom pl)	
sukha	pleasant	
dukkha	unpleasant	
adukkha-m-asukha	neither unpleasant nor pleasant, i e neutral	
ti	so (marks end of quotation)	
katama	what? which?	
pana	but, then	
yaṃ	rel pron nt that which	
kāyika	belonging to the body (kāya m)	
vā ... vā	either ... or	
cetasika	belonging to the mind (ceto nt)	
sāta	sweet, pleasant	
vedeti	know, experience (vedayita p p experienced)	
ayaṃ	that (G 4d)	
asāta	unpleasant	
na eva... na	neither ... nor	
rāga	m passion, desire	
anusaya	m disposition, tendency	
pahātabba	to be abandoned (f p p to pajahāti abandon, get rid of) (G 7c)	[S pra-√hā]
paṭigha	m repulsion	[S prati -√han]
avijjā	f ignorance	[S avidyā]

There are these three feelings: pleasant feeling, unpleasant feeling, neutral feeling.

What is then the pleasant feeling, what is the unpleasant feeling, what is the neutral feeling?

That which is experienced, whether it belongs to the body or the mind (i e whether a material or psychological fact), as pleasant and agreeable, that is pleasant feeling. That which is experienced, whether it belongs to the body or to the mind, as painful and disagreeable, that is an unpleasant feeling. That which is experienced, whether it belongs to the body or to the mind, as neither agreeable nor disagreeable, that is a neutral feeling. A tendency to desire is to be eliminated from the pleasant feeling, a tendency to repulsion is to be eliminated from the unpleasant feeling, a tendency to ignorance is to be eliminated from the neutral feeling.

Notes

This text forms part of a discussion between the nun Dhammadinnā and a layman. The end of the chapter relates how the Buddha himself approves of everything she had said.

According to the Buddhist doctrine, feeling is closely related to the experience of the environment: all impressions that reach our senses are evaluated. Therefore, feelings cannot be avoided; but our text says that they easily give rise to emotional reactions like desire and repulsion, and these have to be checked by the Buddhist. The word anusaya is frequently used in a sense that reminds of the psycho-analytical concept of the unconscious drives.

Neutral feelings easily become ignored, i e unconscious; but this type of feelings are the most useful and should be kept conscious.

(Anguttara Nikaya III 413) Cha y-imā, bhikkhave, saññā: rūpasaññā, saddasaññā, gandhasaññā, rasasaññā, phoṭṭhabbasaññā, dhammasaññā.

(Majjhima Nikaya I 293) Sañjānāti sañjānātīti kho, āvuso, tasmā saññā ti vuccati, kiñ-ca sañjānāti: nīlakam-pi sañjānāti, pītakam-pi sañjānāti, lohitakam-pi sañjānāti, odātam-pi sañjānāti.

cha	six	
ayaṃ	this (imā f nom pl)	
bhikkhu	m monk (voc pl)	
saññā	f perception, idea (nom pl)	
rūpa	nt form	
sadda	m sound	
gandha	m odour	
rasa	m taste	
phoṭṭhabba	nt touchable, touch	[S √spṛś]
dhamma	m idea, mental image	
sañjānāti	recognize, perceive (subject: impersonal)	
ti	so (marks end of quotation)	
kho	indeed	
āvuso	voc pl m friend! (used in polite address)	
tasmā	(abl to so he, that) therefore	
vuccati	is said, is called (pass to vatti, say)	
kiñ = kiṃ	nt what?	
ca	and	
nīlaka	dark blue	
pi	also, even	
pītaka	yellow	
lohitaka	red	
odāta	white	

Monks, there are these six (types of) perceptions: perception of form, of sound, of smell, of taste, of touch, and of ideas.

"One perceives, one perceives", it is said, my friend, therefore it is called "perception". And what does one perceive? One perceives blue, one perceives yellow, one perceives red, one perceives white.

Note

Saññā means about the same as the German "Vorstellung", i e the mental image produced either by direct perception of an object or in the act of remembering or imagining it. The English word "idea" is sometimes used to cover both. In this text, saññā is described mainly as perception, but among the perceptions are also counted the objects of the internal sense, mano, namely dhammā; these are the memory images.

12. THREE TYPES OF ACTIVITY (Majjhima Nikaya I 301)

Tayo 'me sankhārā: kāyasankhāro vacīsankhāro cittasankhāro ti.
Katamo pana kāyasankhāro, katamo vacīsankhāro, katamo cittasankhāro ti?
Assāsā-passāsā kho kāyasankhāro, vitakkavicārā vacīsankhāro, saññā ca vedanā ca cittasankhāro ti.

tayo	m three	[S trayas]
ayaṃ	this (ime m nom pl)	
sankhāra	m activity, energy, process, behaviour	
kāya	m body	
vacī	f speech	
citta	nt mind	
ti	so (marks end of quotation)	
katama	what? which?	
pana	but, now	
assāsa	m exhalation	[S āśvāsa]
passāsa	m inhalation	
kho	indeed	
vitakka	m reasoning, thought, analysis	[S vi-tarka]
vicāra	m cogitation, investigation	
saññā	f perception, ideation	
ca ... ca	both ... and	
vedanā	f feeling	

There are these three (types of) activities: bodily activity, vocal activity and mental activity.
So what is bodily activity, what is vocal activity, what is mental activity?
Exhalation and inhalation are bodily activity, reasoning and investigation are vocal activity, perception and feeling are mental activity.

Notes

This text is part of the same discussion as No. 10.

It is remarkable that thought processes are called an activity of speech. Dr Watson, the well-known behaviorist psychologist, tried to introduce the same idea. Perhaps it was believed that thought processes were always presented psychologically in the form of verbal ideas. From text No. 38, which uses the same words for thought processes, it is anyhow clear that spoken words are not intended.

13. VOLITION AND THE ACTIVITIES (Samyutta Nikaya III 60)

Katamā ca, bhikkhave, sankhārā?

Cha-y-ime, bhikkhave, cetanākāyā: rūpasañcetanā saddasañcetanā gandhasañcetanā rasasañcetanā phoṭṭhabbasañcetanā dhammasañcetanā ime vuccanti, bhikkhave, sankhārā.

katama	what? which? (nom pl m)
ca	and
bhikkhu	m monk (voc pl)
sankhāra	m activity
cha	six
ayaṃ	this (ime m nom pl)
cetanā	f intention, purpose, will
kāya	m body, group, type
rūpa	nt form
sañcetanā	f thought, intention
sadda	m sound
gandha	m odour
rasa	m taste
phoṭṭhabba	nt touch
dhamma	m idea
vuccati	is called (3 pl)

Monks, what are the activities?

Monks, (there are) these six types of volition: striving after form, after sound, after smell, after taste, after touch, after ideas. Monks, these are called activities.

Note

According to the law of karma, rebirth is determined by the activities and their way of influencing consciousness. In this connection we should remember that the activities are conditioned by volition: any particular form of rebirth can be understood as a realization (or, expressed more superficially, as a reward or punishment) of the intentions.

14. THE ORIGIN OF CONSCIOUS PROCESSES (Majjhima Nikaya I 259)

Yañ-ñad-eva, bhikkhave, paccayaṃ paṭicca uppajjati viññāṇaṃ tena ten 'eva sankhaṃ gacchati: cakkhuñ-ca paṭicca rūpe ca uppajjati viññāṇaṃ, cakkhuviññāṇan-t 'eva sankhaṃ gacchati; sotañ-ca paṭicca sadde ca uppajjati viññāṇaṃ, sotaviññāṇan-t 'eva sankhaṃ gacchati; ghānañ-ca paṭicca gandhe ca uppajjati viññāṇaṃ, ghānaviññāṇan-t 'eva sankhaṃ gacchati; jivhañ-ca paṭicca rase ca uppajjati viññāṇaṃ, jivhāviññāṇan-t 'eva sankhaṃ gacchati; kāyañ-ca paṭicca phoṭṭhabbe ca uppajjati viññāṇaṃ, kāyaviññāṇan-t'eva sankhaṃ gacchati; manañ-ca paṭicca dhamme ca uppajjati viññāṇaṃ, manoviññāṇan-t'eva sankhaṃ gacchati.

yañ-ñad = yaṃ yad	whatever	
eva	just, surely	
bhikkhu	m monk (voc pl)	
paccaya	m condition, cause (acc sg)	
paṭicca	conditioned by (ger of pacceti fall back on)	[S pratītya]
uppajjati	arise, be produced	[S ud-√pad]
viññāṇa	nt consciousness	
so	he, that (tena instr sg)	
sankhā	f definition, name	[S sam-√khyā]
gacchati	go; sankhaṃ gacchati be called	
cakkhu	nt eye	[S cakṣus]
ca ··· ca	both ··· and	
rūpa	nt form (acc pl to an implied paṭicca)	
cakkhu-viññāṇa	nt visual consciousness (-an-t 'eva = -aṃ ti eva)	
ti	so (marks end of quotation)	
sota	nt ear	[S śrotas]
sadda	m sound (acc pl)	[S śabda]
ghāna	nt nose	[S ghrāṇa]
gandha	m smell	[S gandha]
jivhā	f tongue	[S jihvā]
rasa	m taste	
kāya	m body	
phoṭṭhabba	nt touch	
mana	nt the internal sense, mind	
dhamma	m idea, mental image	

Monks, from whatever cause consciousness arises, from that it is named: when consciousness arises because of the eye and forms, it is named visual consciousness; when consciousness arises because of the ear and sounds, it is named auditive consciousness; when consciousness arises because of the nose and odours, it is named olfactory consciousness; when consciousness arises because of the tongue and tastes, it is called taste consciousness; when consciousness arises because of the body and contacts, it is called touch consciousness; when consciousness arises because of the internal sense and ideas, it is called consciousness of ideas.

Notes

Yañ-ñad ··· tena tena: a universal relative clause is introduced by a repeated rel pron and the correlative is also repeated. Translate: "whatever cause ··· from that". Yañ-ñad is nt although it evidently belongs to paccayaṃ which is usually m.

cakkhuñ-ca etc: coordinated clauses where we prefer subordination: "when consciousness arises ··· it is named ···"

cakkhu-viññāṇa etc "eye-consciousness", "ear-consciousness", "nose-consciousness" etc: we prefer "visual consciousness" etc. According to Buddhism, there are six senses, the last of which perceives the ideas produced through memory and imagination.

Viññāṇa is a complex concept and difficult to understand completely, as we shall find in later quotations. From this text it becomes clear that viññāṇa, at least in its basic function, is a name for certain information processes conditioned by the senses.

15. CONSCIOUSNESS AND REBIRTH (Anguttara Nikaya I 223)

- Bhavo bhavo ti, bhante, vuccati. Kittāvatā nu kho, bhante, bhavo hotī ti?

- Kāmadhātu-vepakkañ ca, Ānanda, kammaṃ nābhavissa api nu kho kāmabhavo paññāyethā ti?

- No h 'etaṃ, bhante.

- Iti kho, Ānanda, kammaṃ khettaṃ viññāṇaṃ bījaṃ taṇhā sineho; avijjānīvaraṇānaṃ sattānaṃ taṇhāsaṃyojanānaṃ hīnāya dhātuyā viññāṇaṃ patiṭṭhitaṃ. Evaṃ āyatiṃ punabbhavābhinibbatti hoti. Evaṃ kho, Ānanda, bhavo hotī ti.

bhava	m becoming, (re)birth	
ti	so (quotation mark)	
bhante	sir! (polite address to monk)	
vuccati	is said (pass to vatti say)	[S √vac]
kittāvatā	to what extent?	
nu kho	then	
hoti	there is	
kāma	m love, passion, pleasure	
dhātu	f element	
kāmadhātu	f world of sensuality	
vepakka	nt ripening	
ca	and, if	
kamma	nt action	[S karma]
na	not	
bhavati	be (cond 3 sg, "if there had not been") (G 6e)	
api nu	(interrogative particles)	
kāma-bhava	m rebirth in (the world of) sensuality	
pajānāti	know, passive paññāyati (pass 3 sg opt med "would be known") (G 5, 6c)	
no hi etaṃ	certainly not	
iti	so	
khetta	nt field	[S kśetra]
viññāṇa	nt consciousness	
bīja	nt seed	
taṇhā	f thirst, craving	
sineha	m sap; love, desire	[S sneha]
avijjā	f ignorance	

nīvaraṇa	nt obstacle (gen pl)	
satta	m being, creature (gen pl)	
saṃyojana	nt fetter	
hīna	low, miserable, contemptible (loc sg f)	
dhātu	f element, condition (loc sg)	
patiṭṭhita	established, settled (p p to patiṭṭhahati to be set up)	[S prati -√sthā]
evaṃ	so	
āyatiṃ	in future	[S ā-√yam]
punabbhava	m rebirth	
abhinibbatti	f becoming, return	[S abhi-nis-√vṛt]

- "Rebirth, rebirth", it is said, sir. To what extent is there then rebirth, sir?

- Ananda, if there had not been action, ripening in the world of sensuality, would then a rebirth in (the world of) sensuality be known?

- Certainly not, sir.

- In that way, Ananda, action is (like) a field, consciousness (like) a seed and craving (like) sap; for beings that are hindered by ignorance and fettered by craving, consciousness is established on a low level. So rebirth and return is effected in the future. In this way, Ananda, there is rebirth.

Notes

The text is taken from a conversation between the Buddha and his favourite disciple and assistant Ananda. Rebirth is described as a natural consequence of a person's action, kamma (karma). Every action will in due time "ripen" and "bear fruit" in the form of rebirth on a certain level. Three levels are usually mentioned in the literature: kāmadhātu, the world of sensuality, rūpadhātu, the world of form, and arūpadhātu, the formless world. In the process of rebirth, consciousness is "established" on a certain level: it is like a seed that is sown in a certain field; it grows because it has sap or taṇhā (craving). We might compare it to a stream of energy that passes over to a new medium and there produces a new individual. We find also this metaphor in the Pali literature, where the word viññāṇasota, "stream of consciousness", is used.

Kāmadhātuvepakkañ ca: ca may mean "if", but a conditional subordinated clause may also be left without any conditional particle. The compound is possessive and therefore attribute to <u>kamma</u>: "(provided with) sensuality-field-ripening". The compounds <u>avijjānīvaraṇānaṃ</u> and <u>taṇhāsaṃyojanānaṃ</u>, too, are possessive and attributes to <u>sattānaṃ</u>, "ignorance-obstructed" and "craving-bound".

16. CONSCIOUSNESS MAY BE CALMED (Sutta Nipata, verses 734, 735)

Yaṃ kiñci dukkhaṃ sambhoti,
sabbaṃ viññāṇapaccayā,
viññāṇassa nirodhena
n'atthi dukkhassa sambhavo.

Etam ādīnavaṃ ñatvā
"dukkhaṃ viññāṇapaccayā"
viññāṇūpasamā bhikkhu
nicchāto parinibbuto.

yaṃ kiñci	nt whatever
dukkha	nt suffering
sambhoti	arise
sabba	all
viññāṇa	nt consciousness
paccaya	m condition, cause (abl paccayā because of) [S prati-√i]
nirodha	m suppression, ceasing, stilling (instr sg)
na atthi	there is not
sambhava	m origin, production
eso	m esā f etaṃ nt that
ādīnava	m disadvatage, danger
jānāti	know, understand (ñatvā ger, having understood)
upasama	m calming, appeasement (abl sg)
bhikkhu	m monk
nicchāta	satisfied
parinibbuta	released, having attained nirvana

Whatever suffering arises,
it is all because of consciousness.
Through the calming of consciousness
there is no production of suffering.
Having recognized this as a danger,
that suffering is caused by consciousness,
the monk calms his consciousness
and becomes satisfied, attains nirvana.

Notes

The ablatives all indicate the cause or origin: viññāṇūpasamā etc: "from calming (his) consciousness, the monk becomes (bhavati is implied) satisfied ..."

The actions (sankhāra) influence consciousness which accumulates their consequences and is transformed by them, so that the necessary conditions for a new birth are created. In this sense all suffering depends on consciousness. Suffering exists in consciousness, is a conscious fact. Therefore, suffering can cease only if consciousness will cease. The text mentions two expressions for this cessation: nirodha, ceasing, and upasama, appeasement. They both mean the same, because consciousness consists of a stream of processes. The method used in order to make consciousness calm and still, i e to stop the flow of the stream, is called samādhi; if this is successful and followed by complete insight and freedom from disturbing elements (āsava), then nirvana is attained. Since consciousness then is free from all motivation for a change, no rebirth will be possible.

17. THE PSYCHOLOGICAL LAW OF CAUSALITY AND ITS USE (Digha Nikaya I 180 f)

Sahetu sappaccayā purisassa saññā uppajjanti pi nirujjhanti pi. Sikkhā ekā saññā uppajjanti, sikkhā ekā saññā nirujjhanti.

sa	with	
hetu	m cause	
sappaccaya	conditioned	
purisa	m man (gen sg)	
saññā	f idea (nom pl)	
uppajjati	arise (pres 3 pl)	[S ud√pad]
pi ... pi	both ... and	
nirujjhati	cease, disappear (pres 3 pl)	[S ni√rundh]
sikkhā	f training (instr sg)	
ekā ... ekā	some ... others	

The ideas of a man arise and disappear through a cause, through a condition. By means of training some ideas arise, by means of training other ideas disappear.

Notes

sa-hetu with a cause = through a cause, caused;
sa-(p)paccaya with a condition = conditioned.

The goal of Buddhism is attained by means of training, and in this quotation we can learn the basic view behind the training program. Since the stream of consciousness is governed by the causal law, it is possible to produce ideas that lead to development and exclude others.

18. LIBERATION IS A NATURAL PROCESS (Anguttara Nikaya V 2 f)

Sīlavato, bhikkhave, sīlasampannassa na cetanāya karaṇīyaṃ "avippaṭisāro me uppajjatū" ti. Dhammatā esā, bhikkhave, yaṃ sīlavato sīlasampannassa avippaṭisāro uppajjati.

Avippaṭisārissa, bhikkhave, na cetanāya karaṇīyaṃ "pāmujjaṃ me uppajjatū" ti. Dhammatā esā, bhikkhave, yaṃ avippaṭisārissa pāmujjaṃ uppajjati.

Pamuditassa, bhikkhave, na cetanāya karaṇīyaṃ "pīti me uppajjatū" ti. Dhammatā esā, bhikkhave, yaṃ pamuditassa pīti uppajjati.

Pītimanassa, bhikkhave, na cetanāya karaṇīyaṃ "kāyo me passambhatū" ti. Dhammatā esā, bhikkhave, yaṃ pītimanassa kāyo passambhati.

Passaddhakāyassa, bhikkhave, na cetanāya karaṇīyaṃ "sukhaṃ vediyāmī" ti. Dhammatā esā, bhikkhave, yaṃ passaddhakāyo sukhaṃ vediyati.

Sukhino, bhikkhave, na cetanāya karaṇīyaṃ "cittaṃ me samādhiyatū" ti. Dhammatā esā, bhikkhave, yaṃ sukhino cittaṃ samādhiyati.

Samāhitassa, bhikkhave, na cetanāya karaṇīyaṃ "yathābhūtaṃ jānāmi passāmī" ti. Dhammatā esā, bhikkhave, yaṃ samāhito yathābhūtaṃ jānāti passati.

Yathābhūtaṃ, bhikkhave, jānato passato na cetanāya karaṇīyaṃ "nibbindāmi virajjāmī" ti. Dhammatā esā, bhikkhave, yaṃ yathābhūtaṃ jānaṃ passaṃ nibbindati virajjati.

Nibbindassa, bhikkhave, virattassa na cetanāya karaṇīyaṃ "vimuttiñāṇadassanaṃ sacchikaromī" ti. Dhammatā esā, bhikkhave, yaṃ nibbindo viratto vimuttiñāṇadassanaṃ sacchikaroti.

sīlavant	observing the moral rules (sīla nt), virtuous (dat sg)
bhikkhu	m monk (voc pl)
sampanna	endowed with (p p of sampajjati come to); sīla-sampanna endowed with righteousness (dat sg)
na	not
cetanā	f purpose, will (instr)
karaṇīya	what must be done (f p p to karoti make, do); nt need (with instr, "of")
vippaṭisāra	m bad conscience, regret (a-, without) [S vi-prati-√smṛ]
ahaṃ	I (me dat "for me" or loc "in me")

uppajjati	arise (uppajjatu imper 3 sg, may arise),
ti	quotation mark
dhammatā	f conformity to dhamma (nature, rule), natural phenomenon
eso	m esā f etaṃ nt this (nom sg f)
yaṃ	nt rel pron which, that
a-vippaṭisārin	free from regret (adj dat sg, G 3e)
pāmujja	nt joy, happiness, satisfaction [S pra-√mud]
pamudita	p p very pleased (dat sg)
pīti	f delight, joy
mano	nt mind, pīti-mana happy-minded
kāya	m body
me	my (gen to ahaṃ I)
passambhati	calm down, be relaxed (imper 3 sg)
passaddha	p p calmed down, relaxed [S pra-śrabdha]
sukha	nt happiness, pleasure
vediyati	feel, experience (1 sg imper)
sukhin	happy (dat sg)
citta	nt mind
samādahati	concentrate, pass samādhiyati (imper 3 sg pass, "may my mind be concentrated") [S sam-ā-√dhā]
samāhita	p p concentrated (dat sg)
yathābhūtaṃ	as it really is
jānāti	know, understand (imper 1 sg "may I know")
passati	see (imper sg, "may I see")
jānāti	know, pres part jānaṃ knowing (dat sg)
passati	see, pres part passaṃ seeing (dat sg)
nibbindati	get tired of, be disgusted (imper 1 sg, "may I get tired") [S nis-√vid]
virajjati	detach oneself, become free (imper 1 sg, "may I become free") [S vi-√raj]
nibbindati	nibbindo: irregular pres p m nom, dat sg nibbindassa (the regular forms: nibbindaṃ, nibbindato; p p nibbiṇṇa)
virajjati	p p viratta detached, free (dat sg)
vimutti	f release, liberation [S vi-√muc]
ñāṇa	nt knowledge
dassana	nt seeing, insight
sacchikaroti	see, realize (imper 1 sg "may I realize") [S sākṣāt √kṛ]

Monks, for one who is virtuous and follows the ethical norms, there is no need to want, "may freedom from remorse arise in me". Monks, this is in accordance with nature that for one who is virtuous and follows the ethical norms, freedom from remorse arises.

Monks, for one who is free from remorse there is no need to want, "may satisfaction arise in me". Monks, this is in accordance with nature, that for one who is free from remorse satisfaction arises.

Monks, for one who is satisfied there is no need to want, "may joy arise in me". Monks, this is in accordance with nature, that for one who is satisfied joy arises.

Monks, for one who is joyous there is no need to want, "may my body be relaxed". Monks, this is in accordance with nature, that for one who is joyous the body is relaxed.

Monks, for one whose body is relaxed there is no need to want, "may I feel happiness". Monks, this is in accordance with nature, that one whose body is relaxed feels happiness.

Monks, for one who is happy there is no need to want, "may my mind be concentrated". Monks, this is in accordance with nature, that the happy man's mind is concentrated.

Monks, for one who is concentrated, there is no need to want, "may I understand and see as it really is". Monks, this is in accordance with nature, that one who is concentrated understands and sees as it really is.

Monks, for one who understands and sees as it really is, there is no need to want, "may I be disgusted and detach myself". Monks, this is in accordance with nature, that one who understands and sees as it really is becomes disgusted and detaches himself.

Monks, for one who is disgusted and has become detached, there is no need to want, "may I experience the knowledge and insight of liberation". Monks, this is in accordance with nature, that one who is disgusted and has become detached will experience the knowledge and insight of liberation.

Notes

Sīlavato ... na cetanāya karaṇīyaṃ "for the virtuous there is no need to want".

passaddha-kāyassa: possessive compound, "for him who has a relaxed body".

vediyāmi (-ī is sandhi before (i)ti) can be both pres and imper, here imper "may I feel".

The last link of the chain, "knowledge and insight of liberation", refers to nirvana which is described as a state of intellectual clarity in combination with calm satisfaction and internal freedom. The purpose of the text is to show that this ideal state may be attained by means of a causal development in agreement with natural laws, according to which every link naturally leads over to the next. We may note that one of the links is concentration, *samādhi*. This is a meditational state, classed as the last part of the eightfold way. By means of concentration, an ability to more realistic insight and even to supernatural knowledge may be developed.

19. THE ORIGIN AND CONTROL OF SUFFERING (Samyutta Nikaya IV 86)

Cakkhuṃ ca paṭicca rūpe ca uppajjati cakkhuviññāṇaṃ; tiṇṇaṃ sangati phasso; phassapaccayā vedanā; vedanāpaccayā taṇhā; tassā-y-eva taṇhāya asesavirāganirodhā bhavanirodho; bhavanirodhā jātinirodho; jātinirodhā jarāmaraṇaṃ sokaparidevadukkhadomanassupāyāsā nirujjhanti. Evam etassa kevalassa dukkhakkhandhassa nirodho hoti. Ayaṃ dukkhassa atthagamo.

cakkhu	nt eye (acc sg)
ca	and
paṭicca	conditioned by (ger of pacceti fall back on, with acc)
rūpa	nt form, thing (acc pl)
uppajjati	arise
viññāṇa	nt consciousness
cakkhu-viññāṇa	nt visual consciousness
tayo	m tīṇi nt, tisso f three (gen pl nt)
sangati	f meeting, combination
phassa	m contact, stimulation [S sparśa]
paccaya	m condition (abl sg "through")
vedanā	f feeling
taṇhā	f thirst, craving
so	m taṃ nt sā f he, that (gen m nt tassa, gen f tassā)
(y)eva	just, surely
taṇhāya	gen sg of taṇhā
asesa	without remainder, total [S a-śeṣa]
virāga	m indifference, fading away, cleansing
nirodha	m cessation (abl sg)
bhava	m becoming
jāti	f birth
jarā	f old age
maraṇa	nt death
soka	m grief, sorrow
parideva	m lamentation
dukkha	nt suffering
domanassa	nt depression, unhappiness
upāyāsa	m misery, despair (nom pl)

nirujjhati	cease (pres 3 pl)
evaṃ	so
eso	m etaṃ nt esā f this (gen sg m)
kevala	whole (gen sg)
khandha	m group, collection
hoti	is, becomes
ayaṃ m, idaṃ nt, ayaṃ f	this
atthagama	m "going home", going to rest, end

Conditioned by the eye and the forms, visual consciousness arises. The combination of the three is contact (stimulation). Through stimulation (there is) feeling. Through feeling (there is) craving. From the complete fading away and cessation of this craving (there is cessation of becoming =) becoming will end. Through the end of becoming, birth will end. Through the end of birth, old age and death, grief, lamentation, suffering, depression and despair will cease. In this way the cessation of this whole complex of suffering is effected. This is the end of suffering.

Notes

asesa-virāga-nirodhā (abl sg) "from the complete fading away and cessation (of this thirst, gen)".

This "end of suffering" is nirvana. The whole series is a causal explanation of human suffering. The practical application of the series is also pointed out: it offers an opportunity to end suffering. By eliminating one of the early links, we can bring the rest of the chain to disappear. The chain is altogether psychological in the form it is given here: through the perceptual process we see the external world; this process gives rise to feelings, and feelings excite desire; desire is the direct cause of rebirth and suffering.

In the quoted text, the series starts from the visual sense, but the text goes on to repeat the series with the other senses as starting points.

bhava means literally "becoming". It seems to refer to a preliminary stage to jāti,"birth". In Samyutta Nikaya II 4 it is explained as "a preliminary selection of one of the three rebirth-worlds", namely the world of sense-pleasure, the world of form and the formless world.

This text is a variant of a very common series of 12 links, the so-called *paṭiccasamuppāda* series. This starts from *avijjā* "ignorance", and contains some links that are difficult to explain.

20. EVERYTHING IS CAUSED (Samyutta Nikaya I 134)

Yathā aññataraṃ bījaṃ
khette vuttaṃ virūhati
pathavīrasañ cāgamma
sinehañ ca tad ubhayaṃ,
evam khandhā ca dhātuyo
cha ca āyatanā ime
hetuṃ paṭicca sambhūtā
hetubhangā nirujjhare.

yathā ... evaṃ	just as ... so
aññaṭara	a certain, somebody (from añña another, with comparative suffix)
bīja	nt seed
khetta	nt field (loc sg)
vutta	sown (p p to vapati sow)
virūhati	grow, sprout [S vi-√ruh]
pathavī	f earth [S pṛthivī]
rasa	m juice, taste (rasañ = rasaṃ, acc to āgamma)
ca...ca	both... and (ca āgamma)
āgamma	by means of, thanks to (ger to āgacchati come to)
sineha	m sap, fat, moisture
tad	this
ubhaya	both (here nt)
khandha	m personality factor (nom pl)
dhātu	f element (nom pl)
cha	six
āyatana	nt extent, sphere of sense, sense modality
ayaṃ	this (nom pl ime)
hetu	m cause (acc to paṭicca because of)
sambhūta	arisen, produced (p p to sambhavati, arise) (nom pl)
bhanga	nt dissolution (abl sg)
nirujjhati	cease (3 pl pres ind med) (G 5)

Just as a certain seed,
sown in the field, sprouts
because of the earth's juice
and moisture, these two,
so the factors and the elements
and these six sense modalities
are produced through a cause
and cease through the dissolution of the cause.

Notes

The text points out that the human being is produced through causal processes, just as a seed grows because of conditions in the soil.

The personality factors are rūpa, form, body, vedanā, feeling, saññā, perception and ideation, sankhāra, activity, and viññāṇa, consciousness.

The elements are earth, water, fire and air.

The sense modalities are vision, hearing, smell, taste, touch, and the internal sense (a center for the ideation, namely, memory, thinking and imagination).

21. MAN FORMS HIS OWN DESTINY (Dhammapada, verse 80)

Udakaṃ hi nayanti nettikā,
usukārā namayanti tejanaṃ,
dāruṃ namayanti tacchakā,
attānaṃ damayanti paṇḍitā.

udaka	nt water
hi	because, indeed
neti or nayati	lead, conduct (pres 3 pl)
nettika	m one who makes conduits for watering, engineer (nom pl)
usukāra	m arrow-maker, fletcher [S iṣu-√kṛ]
nameti or namayati	bend, wield (pres 3 pl)
tejana	nt arrow
dāru	nt wood
tacchaka	m carpenter [S takṣan]
attā	m self, himself, frequently used as reflexive pron (acc sg) [S ātman]
dameti or damayati	make tame, master (pres 3 pl)
paṇḍita	m wise man (nom pl)

Engineers lead water,
fletchers make arrows,
carpenters form the wood,
wise men master themselves.

Note

tejanaṃ can be understood as collective and therefore translated by plural; attānaṃ: "each his own self", in English plural is the normal way of expressing this.

22. KARMA SOMETIMES WORKS SLOWLY (Dhammapada, verse 71)

Na hi pāpaṃ kataṃ kammaṃ
sajju khīraṃ va muccati;
ḍahaṃ taṃ bālam anveti
bhasmācchanno va pāvako.

na	not	
hi	because, indeed	
pāpa	evil, bad	
kata	done (p p to karoti do, make)	
kamma	nt action (S karman)	
sajju	instantly	[S sadyat]
khīra	nt milk	[S kṣīra]
(i)va	like	
muccati	coagulate, curdle	
ḍahati	burn, ferment (pres part nom)	[S √dah]
so	m taṃ nt sā f he, that	
bāla	ignorant, foolish	
anveti	follow	[S anu-√i]
bhasma	nt ashes	
ācchanna	covered	
pāvaka	m fire	

A bad action that is done,
does not curdle at once, just like milk;
burning it follows the fool
like fire covered by ashes.

Notes

taṃ: probably nt, referring to kammaṃ and subject to anveti, "it"; it could also be understood as definite article to bālam "the fool".

This verse clarifies one aspect of the karma doctrine: every action has consequences for its performer, either in this life or later. The effects may lie hidden, like fire under ashes or like newly drawn milk that does not curdle at once, but they are inescapable.

23. HOW REBIRTH IS INFLUENCED BY ACTIONS (Anguttara Nikaya I 122)

Idha, bhikkhave, ekacco puggalo savyāpajjhaṃ kāyasankhāraṃ abhisankharoti savyāpajjhaṃ vacīsankhāraṃ abhisankharoti savyāpajjhaṃ manosankhāraṃ abhisankharoti. So savyāpajjhaṃ kāyasankhāraṃ abhisankharitvā savyāpajjhaṃ vacīsankhāraṃ abhisankharitvā savyāpajjhaṃ manosankhāraṃ abhisankharitvā savyāpajjhaṃ lokaṃ uppajjati. Taṃ enaṃ savyāpajjhaṃ lokaṃ uppannaṃ samānaṃ savyāpajjhā phassā phusanti. So savyāpajjhehi phassehi phuṭṭho samāno savyāpajjhaṃ vedanaṃ vediyati ekantadukkhaṃ, seyyathāpi sattā nerayikā.

idha	here, in this connection = supposing that
bhikkhu	m monk (voc pl)
ekacca	one, a certain
puggala	m person
savyāpajjha	aggressive (sa- with; vyāpajjha nt harm)
kāya	m body
sankhāra	m activity
abhisankharoti	perform
vacī	f speech
mano	nt the internal sense
so	m he (nt taṃ f sā)
abhisankharitvā	ger having performed
loka	m world
uppajjati	arise, be reborn (here with acc of direction = "to")
taṃ enaṃ	m acc sg "him"
uppanna	reborn (p p to uppajjati)
samāna	being (pres p to atthi is)
phassa	m touch, stimulus, influence (nom pl)
phusati	touch, influence (pres 3 pl)
phassehi	instr pl of phassa
phuṭṭhà	touched, influenced by (p p to phusati) [S √spṛś]
vedanā	f feeling
vediyati	feel
ekanta-	extremely
ekanta-dukkha	extremely painful
seyyathā	just like

api	even
satta	m living being, creature (nom pl)
nerayika	doomed to live in niraya m purgatory

Monks, a certain person here performs aggressive bodily actions, aggressive verbal actions and aggressive mental actions. Having performed aggressive bodily actions, aggressive verbal actions and aggressive mental actions, he is reborn in an aggressive world. When he is reborn in an aggressive world, aggressive stimuli influence him. Being influenced by aggressive stimuli he experiences aggressive feeling that is extremely painful, just like creatures living in Purgatory.

Notes

This text describes one aspect of "karmic" causality. It explains how bad actions are punished and it goes on to describe how good actions are rewarded.

The Buddha mentioned a heaven and a purgatory (often called "hell" in translations): both are places where people are reborn because of their actions. But life even in these places is only temporal and the beings living there must again be reborn according to their actions. The goal of Buddhists is to avoid all kinds of rebirths, even rebirth in heaven.

24. A STRONG WISH MAY INFLUENCE REBIRTH (Majjhima Nikaya III 99 f)

Idha, bhikkhave, bhikkhu saddhāya samannāgato hoti, sīlena samannāgato hoti, sutena samannāgato hoti, cāgena samannāgato hoti, paññāya samannāgato hoti. Tassa evaṃ hoti: Aho vatāhaṃ kāyassa bhedā parammaraṇā khattiyamahāsālānaṃ sahavyataṃ uppajjeyyan ti. So taṃ cittaṃ dahati, taṃ cittaṃ adhiṭṭhāti, taṃ cittaṃ bhāveti; tassa te saṅkhārā ca vihāro c'evaṃ bhāvitā bahulīkatā tatr'uppattiyā saṃvattanti. Ayaṃ, bhikkhave, maggo ayaṃ paṭipadā tatr'uppattiyā saṃvattati.

idha	here, in this connection	
bhikkhu	m monk (bhikkhave voc pl)	
saddhā	f faith	[S śraddhā]
samannāgata	endowed with (+ instr)	
hoti	is, becomes	
sīla	nt virtue	
suta	nt learning (lit "heard", p p of suṇāti hear)	
cāga	m renunciation, generosity	
paññā	f knowledge, wisdom	
evaṃ	so, thus (tassa evaṃ hoti "to him thus becomes" = "the thought strikes him"; tassa: dat sg to so he)	
aho vata	oh dear! alas!	
ahaṃ	I	
kāya	m body (gen sg)	
bheda	m breaking, disintegration (abl sg)	
paraṃ	after (with abl)	
maraṇa	nt death (abl sg)	
khattiya	m nobleman	[S kṣatriya]
mahā-sāla	having great halls (possessive compound), rich	
khattiya-mahāsāla	m wealthy nobleman	
sahavyatā	f companionship	
uppajjati	be reborn (opt 1 sg) (G 6c)	
ti	quotation mark	
so	he	
citta	nt mind, thought	
dahati	put, place, fix	[S √dhā]
adhiṭṭhāti	concentrate (one's attention) on	
bhāveti	develop	

te	these (so, nom pl m)	
sankhāra	m activity, process (nom pl)	
vihāra	m staying, state	[S vi-√hṛ]
ca ... ca	both ... and	
bhāvita	developed (p p to bhāveti)	
bahulīkata	practiced	
tatra	there	
uppatti	f origin, rebirth (dat sg)	
saṃvattati	lead to (dat)	
ayaṃ	m idaṃ nt ayaṃ f this	
magga	m way	[S mārga]
paṭipadā	f way, method	

Monks, here a monk is endowed with faith, is endowed with virtue, is endowed with learning, is endowed with generosity, is endowed with wisdom. It occurs to him: "Would that I might be reborn in companionship with the rich aristocracy after the disintegration of my body after death". He fixes his mind on this, concentrates his mind on this, develops his mind on this. These aspirations and this fixation of his, so developed and practiced, will lead to rebirth there. Monks, this way, this method will lead to rebirth there.

Notes

idha is close to the meaning "assume that..."

So taṃ cittaṃ dahati: cittaṃ dahati, "he fixes his mind" (or "thought"), taṃ "on this" (acc sg nt to so, taṃ, sā "this"). Another possibility is to combine taṃ with cittaṃ and translate "this thought".

sankhāra is a word for processes, especially activity governed by will; vihāra is a fixed state of any type.

khattiya is Pali for S kṣatriya, the warrior caste in ancient India.

The text shows how closely related rebirth is to the wishes of the individual himself. But wishes are effective only if the necessary qualifications are present, i e faith, virtue, knowledge, intelligence. In this way, the internal causal process can be used, either in order to form a new life of a certain type or in order to avoid another rebirth altogether

25. A SUMMARY OF THE WAY (Dhammapada, verse 183)

sabbapāpassa akaraṇam
kusalassa upasampadā
sacittapariyodapanam
etaṃ buddhāna sāsanam.

sabba	all
pāpa	nt evil (gen sg)
karaṇa	nt doing
a-karaṇa	nt not-doing
kusala	skilful, good (gen sg)
upasampadā	f undertaking
sa-	own
citta	nt mind
pariyodapana	nt purification
etaṃ	nt that
buddha	m one who has understood, Buddha (gen pl)
sāsana	nt teaching

To avoid all evil,
to do good,
to purify one's own mind
- that is the teaching of the Buddhas.

Note

buddhāna, usually buddhānaṃ: plural because the Buddha taught that men like himself are born with certain intervals. All Buddhas have the same function and teach the same doctrine.

26. MONK OR NOT? (Majjhima Nikaya III 33)

Pubbe kho ahaṃ, āvuso, agāriyabhūto samāno aviddasu ahosiṃ; tassa me Tathāgato vā Tathāgata-sāvako vā dhammaṃ desesi; tāhaṃ dhammaṃ sutvā Tathāgate saddhaṃ paṭilabhiṃ; so tena saddhāpaṭilābhena samannāgato iti paṭisañcikkhiṃ: Sambādho gharāvāso rajāpatho, abbhokāso pabbajjā; na-y-idaṃ sukaraṃ agāraṃ ajjhāvasatā ekanta-paripuṇṇaṃ ekantaparisuddhaṃ sankhalikhitaṃ brahmacariyaṃ carituṃ; yannūnāhaṃ kesamassuṃ ohāretvā kāsāyāni vatthāni acchādetvā agārasmā anagāriyaṃ pabbajeyyan ti. So kho ahaṃ, āvuso, aparena samayena appaṃ vā bhogakkhandhaṃ pahāya mahantaṃ vā bhogakkhandhaṃ pahāya, appaṃ vā ñātiparivaṭṭaṃ pahāya mahantaṃ vā ñātiparivaṭṭaṃ pahāya, kesamassuṃ ohāretvā kāsāyāni vatthāni acchādetvā agārasmā anagāriyaṃ pabbajiṃ.

pubba	former (pubbe loc before)	
kho	indeed	
ahaṃ	I	
āvuso	voc pl m friend(s)!	
agāriya	m layman	
bhūta	become (p p to bhavati become, be)	
samāna	being (pres p to atthi is)	
aviddasu	ignorant	
ahosiṃ	aor 1 sg to bhavati be	
tassa me	dat sg (nom so he, this ahaṃ I) me, lit "to this me"	
Tathāgata	m lit "thus-gone", so developed (title of the Buddha)	
vā ... vā	either ... or	
sāvaka	m disciple	[S √śru]
dhamma	m the Buddhist doctrine	
deseti	teach (aor 3 sg)	[S √diś]
tāhaṃ = taṃ ahaṃ	(taṃ belongs to dhammaṃ: this doctrine)	
sutvā	having heard (ger to suṇāti hear)	
saddhā	f faith	
paṭilabhati	obtain, get (aor 1 sg)	
so	he, that (refers here to 1st person, "I")	
tena	instr sg to so	
paṭilābha	m obtaining, attainment	
samannāgata	endowed with	[S sam-anu- ā -√gam]

iti	so	
paṭisañcikkhati	reflect (aor 1 sg)	[S prati-sam-√khyā]
sambādha	crowded, narrow, full of hindrances	
ghara	nt house	[S gṛha]
āvāsa	m stay, living	[S ā-√vas]
gharāvāsa	m family life	
rajāpatha	m dusty place (raja nt dust, dirt)	
abbhokāsa	m open air, an open place	
pabbajjā	f ordination, homeless life, monk-life	[S pra-√vraj]
na	not (-y-, sandhi)	
idaṃ	that	
sukara	easy	
agāra	nt house	
ajjhāvasati	inhabit (pres p instr sg)	[S adhi-ā-√vas]
ekanta	extremely	
paripuṇṇa	quite full, complete	[S pari-pūrṇa]
parisuddha	quite pure	
sankha	m conch-shell	[S śankha]
likhita	carved, polished	
brahmàcariya	nt religious life, the good life (acc to carituṃ)	
carati	move, live (inf governed by sukaraṃ)	
nūna	now	
yaṃ nūna ahaṃ + opt	"let me now ..."	
kesa	m hair	[S keśa]
massu	nt beard	[S śmaśru]
ohāreti	cut off (ger: having cut off)	[S ava-√hṛ]
kāsāya	yellow (acc pl nt)	
vattha	nt garment, robe, clothes (acc pl)	[S vastra]
acchādeti	put on (ger)	
agārasmā	from home (abl sg to agāra nt)	
anagāriyā	f homeless state (acc of direction)	
pabbajati	go forth, leave home (opt 1 sg; pabbajiṃ aor 1 sg)	
ti	quotation mark	
so ... ahaṃ	I	
kho	indeed, now	
apara	another, later	
samaya	m time	
appa	small, little	[S alpa]
vā ...` vā	either ... or	
bhoga	m possession, wealth	
Khandha	m mass, bulk	
Bhogakkhandha	m mass of wealth, possessions	
pajahati	leave (ger: pahāya)	[S √hā]
mahant	great, big (acc sg)	

ñāti	m relative	
parivaṭṭa	m circle	[S pari-√vṛt]

Friend, formerly when I was a layman I was ignorant. The Buddha or a disciple of the Buddha taught me the doctrine. Having heard the doctrine I got faith in the Buddha. Filled with this attainment of faith I reflected thus, "Family life is narrow and impure but monk-life is free. It is not easy for one who stays at home to live the good life (so that it becomes) quite full, quite pure, polished like a conch-shell. So let me now shave off hair and beard, put on yellow clothes and go out from home into homelessness". Indeed, friend, after some time I left my wealth, whether it was small or great, I left my circle of relatives, whether it was small or great, I shaved off hair and beard, put on yellow clothes and went out from home into homelessness.

Notes

sukaraṃ ... ajjhāvasatā, lit "easily done ... by (instr) one who inhabits ..."

aparena samayena: instr may be used to express point of time, "at a later time".

The text is taken from a discourse by the Buddha. He describes how he imagines that one of his advanced disciples would think back on how it all started. This situation explains the alternatives which we find in the text: it is left open whether the Buddha himself or one of his disciples has given the instruction, whether his family was big or small, etc.

Afterwards, the text goes on to tell how the new monk learned to live according to the rules, practiced meditation and finally became an arahant (perfect).

27. THE FIRST PART OF THE WAY: RIGHT VIEW (Digha Nikaya II 311 f)

Katamā ca, bhikkhave, sammā-diṭṭhi?

Yaṃ kho, bhikkhave, dukkhe ñāṇaṃ dukkha-samudaye ñāṇaṃ dukkhanirodhe ñāṇaṃ dukkha-nirodha-gāminiyā paṭipadāya ñāṇaṃ, ayaṃ vuccati, bhikkhave, sammā-diṭṭhi.

katama	which?
ca	and
bhikkhu	m monk (voc pl)
sammā	adv rightly
diṭṭhi	f view
ya	rel pron
kho	indeed
dukkha	nt suffering (loc sg)
ñāṇa	nt knowledge, understanding
samudaya	m origin (loc)
nirodha	m cessation (loc)
gāmin	going (to gacchati, go), here loc sg f
paṭipadā	f way (loc sg)
vuccati	is said (pass to vatti say)

Monks, what is right view?

Monks, the knowledge about suffering, the knowledge about the origin of suffering, the knowledge about the cessation of suffering, and the knowledge about the way that goes to the cessation of suffering, this, monks, is called right view.

Notes

Yaṃ corresponds to ayaṃ: yaṃ ··· ñāṇaṃ ··· ayaṃ "the knowledge that is about (loc) ··· that is called"; yaṃ agrees with ñāṇaṃ and is nom sg nt, ayaṃ agrees with diṭṭhi (nom sg f).

28. RIGHT PURPOSE (Digha Nikaya II 312)

Katamo ca, bhikkhave, sammā-sankappo?
Nekkhamma-sankappo avyāpāda-sankappo avihiṃsā-sankappo, ayaṃ vuccati, bhikkhave, sammāsankappo.

katama	which?
ca	and
bhikkhu	m monk (voc pl)
sammā	adv rightly
sankappa	m intention, purpose, decision
nekkhamma	nt renunciation
a-vyāpāda	m non-violence, i e kindness
a-vihiṃsā	f freedom from cruelty, harmlessness, compassion
ayaṃ	that
vuccati	is called

Monks, what is right purpose?
The purpose to be free from craving, the purpose not to harm, the purpose not to be cruel - this, monks, is called right purpose.

Note

The formulation in Pali is negative, and we have translated accordingly. It should, however, not be forgotten that negative formulations of this type have a positive meaning: independence, kindness, compassion. In Buddhism, purpose and will as basic traits of character are considered very important. A word for this is sankappa. Our quotation defines the core of Buddhist ethics.

29. RIGHT SPEECH (Digha Nikaya II 312)

Katamā ca, bhikkhave, sammā-vācā?

Musā-vādā veramaṇī, pisuṇāya vācāya veramaṇī, pharusāya vācāya veramaṇī, samphappalāpā veramaṇī, ayaṃ vuccati, bhikkhave, sammā--vācā.

katama	which?	
ca	and	
bhikkhu	m monk (voc pl)	
sammā	adv rightly	
vācā	f speech	
musā	adv falsely	[S mṛṣā]
vāda	m speech (abl sg)	
veramaṇī	f abstention (+ abl "from")	
pisuṇa	malicious (abl sg f)	
pharusa	harsh, rough (abl sg f)	
sampha	frivolous, foolish	
palāpa	m prattle, gossip	
ayaṃ	that	
vuccati	is called	

Monks, what is right speech?

To refrain from false speech, to refrain from malicious talk, to refrain from unkind talk, to refrain from thoughtless gossip - that, monks, is called right speech.

30. A MORE DETAILED DEFINITION OF RIGHT SPEECH (Anguttara Nikaya V 205)

Musāvādaṃ pahāya musāvādā paṭivirato hoti, saccavādī saccasandho theto paccayiko avisaṃvādako lokassa, pisuṇaṃ vācaṃ pahāya pisuṇāya vācāya paṭivirato hoti; na ito sutvā amutra akkhātā imesaṃ bhedāya, amutra vā sutvā na imesaṃ akkhātā amūsaṃ bhedāya; iti bhinnānaṃ vā sandhātā sahitānaṃ vā anuppadātā samaggārāmo samaggarato samagganandī samaggakaraṇiṃ vācaṃ bhāsitā hoti. Pharusaṃ vācaṃ pahāya pharusāya vācāya paṭivirato hoti, yā sā vācā nelā kaṇṇasukhā pemanīyā hadayangamā porī bahujanakantā bahujanamanāpā, tathārūpiṃ vācaṃ bhāsitā hoti. Samphappalāpaṃ pahāya samphappalāpā paṭivirato hoti kālavādī bhūtavādī atthavādī dhammavādī vinayavādī, nidhānavatiṃ vācaṃ bhāsitā hoti kālena sāpadesaṃ pariyantavatiṃ atthasaṃhitaṃ.

musā-vāda	m false speech	
pajahati	leave, refrain from (ger)	
paṭivirata	abstaining from (p p to paṭiviramati abstain from)	
hoti	is	
sacca	nt truth	
vādin	speaking (nom sg) (G 3c)	
saccasandha	truthful, reliable	
theta	firm, reliable	[S sthātṛ]
paccayika	trustworthy	[S pratyaya]
a-visaṃvādaka	not deceiving	[S vi-sam-√vad]
loka	m world, people (gen sg)	
pisuṇa	malicious	
vācā	f speech	
na	not	
ito	(from) here	
suṇāti	hear (sutvā ger having heard)	
amutra	there	
akkhātar	m one who relates (nom sg)	[S ā-√khyā]
imesaṃ	gen pl of ayaṃ this	
bheda	m breaking, dissension (dat sg)	
vā	or	
amūsaṃ	gen pl of asu that one	
iti	thus	
bhinna	broken, discordant (p p to bhindati break)	
vā ... vā	either ... or	

sandhātar	m one who puts together, a conciliator (nom sg)	
sahita	united (gen pl)	
anuppadātar	m one who effects (nom sg)	[S anu-pra-√dā]
samagga	harmonious; nt peace	
ārāma	m delight	
samaggārāma	rejoicing in peace	
samaggarata	delighting in peace (rata delighting in)	
nandin	rejoicing, happy (nom sg)	
karaṇa	producing (iṃ acc sg f)	
bhāsitar	m one who speaks	
pharusa	harsh, rough	
yā sā	just such as (nom fem)	
nela	faultless, gentle, merciful	
kaṇṇa	m ear	[S karṇa]
kaṇṇa-sukha	pleasant to hear	
pemanīya	affectionate, kind	[S √prī]
hadaya	m heart	[S hṛdaya]
gama	going	
hadayangama	heart-stirring, agreeable	
porin	polite (nom sg)	
bahu	much, many	
jana	m person, people (collective sg)	
kanta	agreeable ("agreeable to many people")	
manāpa	pleasing ("pleasing to many people")	
tathārūpi	such, lit "of such form" (rūpa)	
sampha	frivolous, foolish	
palāpa	m prattle, gossip	
kāla	m time	
kāla-vādin	speaking at the proper time	
bhūta	nt truth (p p to bhavati become)	
attha	m thing, sense, profit	
dhamma	m doctrine	
vinaya	m discipline, norm	
nidhānavant	worth treasuring, worth remembering (acc sg f)	
sāpadesa	with reasons, well-grounded	
pariyantavant	purposeful, discriminating	
attha-saṃhita	useful, profitable	

He (i e the Buddhist monk) gives up false speech and refrains from false speech; he speaks the truth, is reliable, firm and trustworthy and does not deceive people. He gives up malicious talk and abstains from malicious talk; if he has heard anything here, he will not tell it elsewhere in order to cause dissension with these (i e the people here); or if he has heard something there, he will not tell it to the people here in order to cause dissension with the people on the other place. Thus he becomes either a conciliator of enemies or a creator of friends (or maybe: a supporter of the friendly). He rejoices in peace, delights in peace, finds happiness in peace and speaks words that make for peace. He gives up unkind talk and refrains from unkind talk; but such words as are gentle, pleasant to hear, kind, heart-stirring, polite, agreeable to many people, pleasing to many people, such words he will speak. He gives up foolish gossip and refrains from foolish gossip; he speaks at the proper time, he speaks the truth, he speaks what is useful, he speaks about the doctrine, about the rules; at the proper time he will speak words that are worth remembering, well-grounded, purposeful and profitable.

Notes

imesaṃ bhedāya "in order to create dissension with these"; bhedāya dat indicating purpose, imesaṃ gen pl "with these", i e the people on the place where he heard the rumours; amūsaṃ bhedāya: "in order to create dissension with those", i e with the people on the other place; ayaṃ refers to somebody near to the speaker, asu to somebody far from the speaker.

bhāsitā hoti, lit "becomes a speaker (of words)"

Vinaya, "rule", is the name of the collection of rules by which the life of the monks is regulated.

31. RIGHT ACTION (Digha Nikaya II 312)

Katamo ca, bhikkhave, sammā - kammanto?

Pāṇātipātā veramaṇī adinnādānā veramaṇī, kāmesu micchācārā veramaṇī, ayaṃ vuccati, bhikkhave, sammā-kammanto.

katama	which?	
ca	and	
bhikkhu	m monk (voc pl)	
sammā	adv rightly	
kammanta	m work, action	
pāṇa	m breath, life	[S prāṇa]
atipāta	m killing (abl sg)	
veramaṇī	f abstention (+ abl "from")	
a-dinna	p p not given (dinna p p to dadāti give)	
ādāna	nt taking (abl sg)	
adinn'ādāna	taking what has not been given, i e theft	
kāma	m sense-pleasures, here: sexual love (loc pl)	
micchā	adv wrongly	
cāra	m behaviour	
kāmesu micchācārā	(abl sg) sexual misconduct	
ayaṃ	that	
vuccati	is called	

Monks, what is right action?

To refrain from killing life, to refrain from taking what has not been given, to refrain from sexual misconduct - that, monks, is called right action.

32. HOW THE PERFECT ONES LIVE (Anguttara Nikaya I 211 f)

Yāvajīvaṃ arahanto abrahmacariyaṃ pahāya brahmacārī ārācārī viratā methunā gāmadhammā.

Yāvajīvaṃ arahanto surā-meraya-majja-pamādaṭṭhānaṃ pahāya surā-meraya-majja-pamādaṭṭhānā paṭiviratā.

Yāvajīvaṃ arahanto ekabhattikā rattūparatā viratā vikālabhojanā.

Yāvajīvaṃ arahanto nacca-gīta-vādita-visūka-dassanā mālā-gandha-vilepana-dhāraṇa-maṇḍana-vibhūsanaṭṭhānā paṭiviratā.

Yāvajīvaṃ arahanto uccāsayana-mahāsayanaṃ pahāya uccāsayana-mahāsayanā paṭiviratā nīcaseyyaṃ kappenti mañcake vā tiṇasanthārake vā.

yāva	as long as	
jīva	m life	
yāvajīvaṃ	adv life-long	
arahant	m worthy one, perfected one	
a-brahmacariya	nt immoral life, unchastity	
pajahati	leave (pahāya ger "having abandoned")	
brahmacārin	leading a pure life (nom pl)	
ārā	far from	
ārā-cārin	living far (from evil)	
virata	abstaining from (+ abl) (nom pl)	
methuna	nt sexual intercourse (abl sg)	
gāma	m village	[S grāma]
dhamma	m thing, behaviour, mentality (gāma-dhamma "village-behaviour", is said to mean "intercourse with women")	
surā	f intoxicating liquor	
meraya	nt alcoholic drink	
majja	nt intoxication	[S madya]
pamāda	m indolence	[S pra-√mad]
ṭhāna	nt state (abl sg)	[S √sthā]
paṭivirata	abstaining from (+ abl)	
eka	one, only one	
bhatta	nt food, meal	[S bhakta]
ekabhattika	eating only one meal (adj nom pl)	
ratta	nt night, time	
uparata	abstaining from	

rattūparata	abstaining from food at night (nom pl)	
vikāla	m "wrong time", i e afternoon	
bhojana	nt food	
vikālabhojana	taking a meal at the wrong time, i e in the afternoon	
nacca	nt dancing	[S natya]
gīta	nt singing	
vādita	nt instrumental music	
visūka	nt performance	
dassana	nt seeing	[S darśana]
mālā	f garland	
gandha	m perfume	
vilepana	nt ointment, cosmetic	[S √lip]
dhāraṇa	nt wearing	
maṇḍana	nt ornament	
vibhūsana	nt adornment	
vibhūsanaṭṭhāna	"state of being adorned"	
uccā-	(only in compounds) high	
sayana	nt bed	
mahant	great, big (mahā: one of the stem forms used in compounds)	
nīca	low, humble	
seyyā	f bed	
kappeti	prepare, arrange (3 pl)	
mañcaka	m bed, pallet (loc sg)	
vā ... vā	either ... or	
tiṇa	nt grass	[S tṛṇa]
santhāraka	m mat (loc sg)	

As long as they live the perfected ones abandon unchastity: they live a pure life, far from evil, and abstain from sexual intercourse and village-behaviour.

As long as they live the perfected ones abandon the state of indolence caused by intoxication with alcoholic drinks and liquor and abstain from the state of indolence caused by intoxication with alcoholic drinks and liquor.

As long as they live the perfected ones live on one meal (a day), abstaining from food at night, refraining from food at improper times.

As long as they live the perfected ones refrain from seeing performances of dancing, singing and instrumental music and from dressing up and adorning themselves by using garlands, perfumes and cosmetics.

As long as they live the perfected ones avoid (using) a high bed or a wide bed and refrain from a high bed or a wide bed. They prepare a low bed either on a pallet or on a mat of grass.

Notes

The long compound _mālā ··· ṭṭhānā_ should first be analyzed into two halves. Each half begins with a number of coordinated nouns which are objects to a verbal noun. The relation between the two halves may be understood in two ways: a) coordination: "(abstaining from) wearing ··· _and_ from the state of being dressed up and adorned" b) instrumental subordination: "(abstaining from) the state of being dressed up and adorned _through_ wearing garlands ..."

It should be noted that the _arahant_, "who has done what was to be done" and attained the goal, continues to lead the simple and disciplined life of his training.

33. RIGHT LIVELIHOOD (Digha Nikaya II 312)

Katamo ca, bhikkhave, sammā-ājīvo?

Idha, bhikkhave, ariya-sāvako micchā-ājīvaṃ pahāya sammā-ājīvena jīvikaṃ kappeti, ayaṃ vuccati, bhikkhave, sammā-ājīvo.

katama	which?
ca	and
bhikkhu	m monk (voc pl)
sammā	adv rightly
ājīva	m livelihood
idha	here
ariya	noble
sāvaka	m disciple
micchā	adv falsely
pajahati	abandon (ger)
jīvikā	f living, livelihood
kappeti	prepare, find, get
ayaṃ	this
vuccati	is called

Monks, what is right livelihood?

Monks, with regard to this a disciple of the noble ones avoids wrong livelihood and obtains his means of living through right livelihood - this, monks, is called right livelihood.

34. WRONG LIVELIHOOD (Majjhima Nikaya III 75)

Katamo ca, bhikkhave, micchā-ājīvo?
Kuhanā lapanā nemittakatā nippesikatā lābhena lābhaṃ nijigiṃsanatā, ayaṃ, bhikkhave, micchā-ājīvo.

katama	which?
ca	and
bhikkhu	m monk (voc pl)
micchā	adv wrongly
ājīva	m livelihood
kuhanā	f deceit
lapanā	f speech, prattling
kuhanā lapanā	deceitful talk, or: deceit and cajolery
nemittakatā	f soothsaying (nemitta m fortune-teller)
nippesikatā	f trickery, humbug
lābha	m acquisition, gain (lābhena instr sg)
nijigiṃsanatā	f covetousness, rapacity: "greediness for gain upon gain"
ayaṃ	this

Monks, what is wrong livelihood?
Deceitful talk, soothsaying, humbug, greediness for gain upon gain - this, monks, is wrong livelihood.

35. RIGHT EFFORT (Digha Nikaya II 312)

Katamo ca, bhikkhave, sammā-vāyāmo?

Idha, bhikkhave, bhikkhu anuppannānaṃ pāpakānaṃ akusalānaṃ dhammānaṃ anuppādāya chandaṃ janeti vāyamati, viriyaṃ ārabhati, cittaṃ paggaṇhāti padahati. Uppannānaṃ pāpakānaṃ akusalānaṃ dhammānaṃ pahānāya chandaṃ janeti vāyamati, viriyaṃ ārabhati, cittaṃ paggaṇhāti padahati. Anuppannānaṃ kusalānaṃ dhammānaṃ uppādāya chandaṃ janeti vāyamati, viriyaṃ ārabhati, cittaṃ paggaṇhāti padahati. Uppannānaṃ kusalānaṃ dhammānaṃ ṭhitiyā asammosāya bhiyyobhāvāya vepullāya bhāvanāya pāripūriyā chandaṃ janeti vāyamati, viriyaṃ ārabhati, cittaṃ paggaṇhāti padahati. Ayaṃ vuccati, bhikkhave, sammā-vāyāmo.

katama	which?
ca	and
bhikkhu	m monk (voc pl)
sammā	adv rightly
vayama	m effort
idha	here
an-uppanna	not arisen (gen pl); uppanna arisen (p p to uppajjati be produced)
pāpaka	bad, evil (gen pl)
a-kusala	improper, not suitable (gen pl); kusala skilful, appropriate
dhamma	m idea, psychological state or process (gen pl)
an-uppāda	m non-appearance (dat sg)
chanda	m intention, will
janeti	produce, cause
vāyamati	endeavour, strive
viriya	nt energy
ārabhati	begin, undertake
viriyaṃ ārabhati	make an effort
citta	nt mind
paggaṇhāti	stretch forth, exert, strain
padahati	exert
pahāna	nt abandoning, rejection (dat sg "in order to drive away")
uppāda	m appearance (dat sg)

ṭhiti	f state, persistence, stabilizing (dat sg)
a-sammosa	m absence of confusion (dat sg)
bhiyyo-bhāva	m becoming (bhāva) more (bhiyyo), increase (dat sg)
vepulla	nt abundance, fullness (dat sg)
bhāvanā	f developing, cultivation (dat sg)
pāripūrī	f completion (dat sg)
ayaṃ	this
vuccati	is called

Monks, what is right effort?

Monks, with regard to this the monk makes a resolution and an effort, mobilizes energy, concentrates and forces his mind, in order that evil and inappropriate mental processes, that have not yet arisen, may not be produced. He makes a resolution and an effort, mobilizes energy, concentrates and forces his mind, in order to expell evil and inappropriate mental processes that have already arisen. He makes a resolution and an effort, mobilizes energy, concentrates and forces his mind in order that skilful mental processes, that have not yet arisen, may be produced. He makes a resolution and an effort, mobilizes energy, concentrates and forces his mind in order that skilful mental processes that have already arisen may be stabilized, gain clarity, reach full growth, development and completeness.

Monks, this is called right effort.

Notes

anuppādāya, dat sg "for the non-appearance of" (+ gen pl), a way of expressing purpose; we would say: "in order that evil and inappropriate mental processes that have not arisen may not be produced".

The word dhamma is used in many senses; one of the most common is "idea", "mental image", "conscious content", "conscious process". In this context it is usually translated by "state". However, the Buddha's view of personality was dynamic. He found no states, only processes. Strictly, only nirvana is a state, i e something static. What is meant here is the stream of mental contents or processes: images, feelings, wishes, of which some lead to development (they are "skilful"), others to deterioration (they are "inappropriate").

The Buddha's view of the internal processes was causal: every process is caused by another process and will itself give rise to a further process, and so on. Since this was true also on the ethical plane, every process could be viewed as "reward" or "punishment" of an earlier process, just as motor trouble can be viewed as a "punishment" for taking bad care of the car. Therefore, our moral development and our future in general is a natural consequence of the nature of the internal processes; so it is not necessary to call them "good" or "bad". In fact, these words are often replaced by <u>kusala</u> and <u>akusala</u>, i e "skilful" and "unskilled", or "appropriate" and "inappropriate".

36. RIGHT MINDFULNESS (Digha Nikaya II 292)

Bhikkhu gacchanto vā "Gacchāmīti" pajānāti, ṭhito vā "Ṭhito'mhīti" pajānāti, nisinno vā "Nisinno 'mhīti" pajānāti, sayāno vā "Sayāno 'mhīti" pajānāti. Yathā yathā vā pan'assa kāyo paṇihito hoti, tathā tathā naṃ pajānāti.

Iti ajjhattaṃ vā kāye kāyānupassī viharati, bahiddhā vā kāye kāyānupassī viharati, ajjhatta-bahiddhā vā kāye kāyānupassī viharati. Samudaya-dhammānupassī vā kāyasmiṃ viharati, vaya-dhammānupassī vā kāyasmiṃ viharati, samudaya-vaya-dhammānupassī vā kāyasmiṃ viharati. "Atthi kāyo" ti vā pan'assa sati paccupaṭṭhitā hoti yāvad eva ñāṇa-mattāya paṭissati-mattāya. Anissito ca viharati na ca kiñci loke upādiyati.

Gate ṭhite nisinne sutte jāgarite bhāsite tuṇhībhāve sampajana-kārī hoti.

bhikkhu	m monk
gacchati	go (gacchanto pres part nom sg "going")
vā ··· vā	either ··· or
iti	so (ends quotation)
pajānāti	know
ṭhita	standing, upright (p p of tiṭṭhati stand)
amhi	I am
ṭhito'mhi	I am standing
nisinna	sitting (p p of nisīdati sit)
sayāna	lying down (pres p med of sayati lie down)
yathā yathā ... tathā tathā	however ··· so
vā	or
pana	further
assa	his (gen sg to so he)
kāya	m body
paṇihita	placed, directed (p p to paṇidahati, put down, direct)
hoti	is
naṃ	it (acc sg of pron eso this)
iti	so
ajjhattaṃ	adv inwardly, introspectively
anupassin	observing (nom sg)

viharati	stay, continue
bahiddhā	adv outside, externally
samudaya	m origination
dhamma	m phenomenon, thing
kāya	m body (loc sg)
vaya	m loss, decay
atthi	there is
sati	f mindfulness, consciousness
assa	dat and gen sg m to ayaṃ this
paccupaṭṭhita	p p established, present
yāvad eva	at least, as far as
ñāṇa	nt understanding
mattā	f measure (mattāya dat sg "for the purpose of") [S mātrā]
paṭissati	f memory, mindfulness [S prati-√smṛ]
anissita	independent [S a-niśrita]
na kiñci	nt nothing
loka	m world (loc sg)
upādiyati	cling to, grasp
gata	gone (p p of gacchati go; absolute loc = "when he goes")
ṭhite	when he stands
nisinne	when he sits
supati	sleep (sutte p p loc sg, when he sleeps) [S √svap]
jāgarati	be awake (jāgarite p p loc sg, when he is awake)
bhāsati	speak (bhāsite p p loc sg, when he speaks)
tuṇhī-bhāva	m silence (loc sg) [S tūṣṇīm]
sampajāna	attentive, conscious
kārin	making, acting; sampajāna-kārin, acting with full attention

When going, the monk knows "I am going", or, when standing, he knows "I am standing", or, when sitting, he knows "I am sitting", or, when lying down, he knows "I am lying down". Or in whatever position his body is placed, he is aware of it.

So he continues to observe the body in the body inwardly, or he continues to observe the body in the body externally, or he continues to observe the body in the body both inwardly and externally. He continues to observe growth-tendencies in the body, or he continues to observe decay-tendencies in the body, or he continues to observe tendencies to both growth and decay in the body. But so is established in him the consciousness "There is the body", at least enough for understanding and mindfulness. And he remains independent and does not cling to anything in the world.

Whether he goes, stands or sits, sleeps or is awake, speaks or is silent, he is acting with full attention.

Notes

kāye kāyānupassī has been translated in different ways. The PTS Dictionary gives the translation "contemplating the body as an accumulation". This does not seem satisfactory, since the text uses parallel expressions about the mind and the feelings: citte cittānupassī, vedanāsu vedanānupassī. The English translation by T.W. and C.A.F. Rhys Davids says "So does he, as to the body, continue to consider the body". In this translation, kāye is understood as the locative expressing reference. This is not an uncommon function and the interpretation may be correct. Another literal translation would be "observing the body in the body", whatever that means. It may be just an idiom for concentrated attention. Or one might be reminded of a phrase in Udana p 8: diṭṭhe diṭṭhamattaṃ bhavissati "in the seen, there shall be just the seen". We could translate this passage in a similar way, "considering the body as body (and nothing else)". This translation would be in good agreement with the Buddhist recommendation to avoid feelings and involvement with regard to things perceived.

ajjhattaṃ ... bahiddhā, "internally - externally", probably means, "from the inside (by calling to mind all kinds of internal sensations from the body) ... from the outside (by calling to mind all external aspects of the body)".

The basic idea in the sati-exercises here described is that the bodily or mental processes should be closely followed by means of conscious observation. In this way, consciousness is focussed on the present moment and on the personal phenomena. This self-observation is practiced until it becomes a habit. In this way, the person learns to know himself and to expell from his mind everything that is distant or disturbing. It is a method that finally leads to full control over the conscious processes and so to freedom from dependence and freedom from anxiety.

37. IRRADIATION OF FRIENDLINESS, COMPASSION, TENDERNESS, AND EQUANIMITY (Digha Nikaya III 223 f)

Idh´, āvuso, bhikkhu mettā-sahagatena cetasā ekaṃ disaṃ pharitvā viharati, tathā dutiyaṃ, tathā tatiyaṃ, tathā catutthiṃ. Iti uddham adho tiriyaṃ sabbadhi sabbatthatāya sabbāvantaṃ lokaṃ mettā-sahagatena cetasā vipulena mahaggatena appamāṇena averena avyāpajjhena pharitvā viharati.

Karuṇā-sahagatena cetasā ekaṃ disaṃ pharitvā viharati, tathā dutiyaṃ, tathā tatiyaṃ, tathā catutthiṃ. Iti uddham adho tiriyaṃ sabbadhi sabbatthatāya sabbāvantaṃ lokaṃ karuṇā-sahagatena cetasā vipulena mahaggatena appamāṇena averena avyāpajjhena pharitvā viharati.

Muditā-sahagatena cetasā ekaṃ disaṃ pharitvā viharati, tathā dutiyaṃ, tathā tatiyaṃ, tathā catutthiṃ. Iti uddham adho tiriyaṃ sabbadhi sabbatthatāya sabbāvantaṃ lokaṃ muditā-sahagatena cetasā vipulena mahaggatena appamāṇena averena avyāpajjhena pharitvā viharati.

Upekhā-sahagatena cetasā ekaṃ disaṃ pharitvā viharati, tathā dutiyaṃ, tathā tatiyaṃ, tathā catutthiṃ. Iti uddham adho tiriyaṃ sabbadhi sabbatthatāya sabbāvantaṃ lokaṃ upekhā-sahagatena cetasā vipulena mahaggatena appamāṇena averena avyāpajjhena pharitvā viharati.

idha	here, now	
āvuso	voc pl, friends!	
bhikkhu	m monk	
mettā	f friendliness, sympathy	[S maitra]
sahagata	"gone with", filled with (instr sg)	
ceto	nt mind (instr sg)	
eka	one	
disā	f direction, quarter	
pharati	pervade, fill (ger)	
viharati	remain, continue	
tathā	so, then	
dutiya	second	[S dvitīya]
tatiya	third	[S tṛtīya]
catuttha	fourth (here: acc fem, ending in -ī)	[S caturtha]
iti	so	
uddhaṃ	up, above	[S ūrdhva]
adho	down, below	[S adhas]

tiriyaṃ	horizontally
sabbadhi	everywhere, in all directions
sabbatthatā	f the state of being everywhere (derived from sabbattha everywhere). Here loc: "everywhere"
sabbāvant	whole, all (acc sg)
loka	m world
vipula	large, abundant (instr sg)
mahaggata	"become (gata) great (mahant)", enlarged
appamāṇa	immeasurable, endless
avera	free from hate, mild, friendly [S vaira hate]
avyāpajjha	not injuring, kind
karuṇā	f compassion
muditā	f kindliness, gentleness, tenderness
upekhā	f neutrality, equanimity [S upa- √iks]

Friends, now the monk remains pervading one quarter, then a second, then a third and a fourth, with a mind filled with friendliness. Up, down, horizontally: in all directions, everywhere, he goes on pervading the whole world with a mind filled with friendliness, extensive, expanded, boundless, free from hate and malevolence.

He remains pervading one quarter, then a second, then a third and a fourth, with a mind filled with compassion. Up, down, horizontally: in all directions, everywhere, he goes on pervading the whole world with a mind filled with compassion, extensive, expanded, boundless, free from hate and malevolence.

He remains pervading one quarter, then a second, then a third and a fourth, with a mind filled with tenderness. Up, down, horizontally: in all directions, everywhere, he goes on pervading the whole world with a mind filled with tenderness, extensive, expanded, boundless, free from hate and malevolence.

He remains pervading one quarter, then a second, then a third and a fourth, with a mind filled with equanimity. Up, down, horizontally: in all directions, everywhere, he goes on pervading the whole world with a mind filled with equanimity, extensive, expanded, boundless, free from hate and malevolence.

Notes

pharitvā viharati, lit "he remains having pervaded ..." Viharati is often used together with ger and is then to be considered as an auxiliary verb expressing duration or continuous action. So translate "he remains pervading", "he goes on filling".

A person practicing meditation may experience an expansion of his consciousness, and a direct contact with the whole world is felt to be possible. In the exercise here described, the mind is brought to function in about the same way as a radio transmitter: radiations of friendliness, compassion, tenderness, and equanimity are transmitted in every direction.

38. THE FIRST OF THE NINE LEVELS OF CONCENTRATION
(Digha Nikaya I 182)

So vivicc'eva kāmehi vivicca akusalehi dhammehi savitakkaṃ savicāraṃ vivekajaṃ pīti-sukhaṃ paṭhamajjhānam upasampajja viharati. Tassa yā purimā kāma-saññā sā nirujjhati. Vivekaja-pīti-sukha-sukhuma-sacca-saññā tasmiṃ samaye hoti, vivekaja-pīti-sukha-sukhuma-sacca-saññī yeva tasmiṃ samaye hoti.

so	he	
vivicca	+ abl, separated from	
eva	even	
kāma	m, nt sense-desire, sensual pleasure (abl pl)	
akusala	improper, unskilled (abl pl)	
dhamma	m thing, idea, conscious process (abl pl)	
sa-	with	
vitakka	m thinking, reflection	
vicāra	m investigation, examination	
viveka	m detachment, seclusion	
-ja	born, produced	
pīti	f joy, delight	[S prīti]
sukha	nt happiness	
paṭhama	first	
jhāna	nt meditation	[S dhyāna]
upasampajjati	attain (ger)	[S -padya]
viharati	remain, continue	
so	he (tassa gen sg)	
yā ... sā	that which ... that (f nom)	
purima	former, earlier	
saññā	f perception, consciousness	
nirujjhati	be dissolved, cease	
sukhuma	subtle, just noticeable	[S sūkṣma]
sacca	true, real	
so	that (tasmiṃ loc sg)	
samaya	m time (loc sg)	
hoti	is, becomes	
saññin	conscious (nom sg m)	
(y)eva	even, just	

Free from sense-desires and free from improper mental contents he enters and remains in the first meditation, a state of joy and happiness, born of seclusion, combined with analytic and investigating thought processes. The consciousness of desire which he formerly had, disappears. A subtle but real awareness of joy and happiness, born of seclusion, arises at that time and he becomes at that time subtly but truly aware of joy and happiness, born of seclusion.

Notes

jhāna is a name for the first four levels of concentration. They are said to have been practiced before the time of the Buddha, and taken over by him.

The exact meaning of vitakka and vicāra is not very well known. They both refer to thought processes of a more analytical and differentiated type, working with details, and are therefore differentiated from paññā which refers to a synthetic and intuitive understanding. They both mean thinking as problem solving. Probably vitakka implies a first analytical phase of attention in which the problem is perceived and analyzed, while vicāra refers to a later, experimenting phase in which the relations between the parts are further explored.

Since texts No. 38-43 form a unit and to a great extent use the same vocabulary, the words are explained only once.

39. THE SECOND LEVEL OF CONCENTRATION (Digha Nikaya I 182)

Puna ca paraṃ bhikkhu vitakka-vicārānaṃ vūpasamā ajjhattaṃ sampasādanaṃ cetaso ekodibhāvaṃ avitakkaṃ avicāraṃ samādhijaṃ pīti-sukhaṃ dutiyajjhānaṃ upasampajja viharati.

Tassa yā purimā vivekajaṃ pīti-sukhaṃ sukhuma-sacca-saññā sā nirujjhati. Samādhija-pīti-sukha-sukhuma-sacca-saññā tasmiṃ samaye hoti, samādhija-pīti-sukha-sukhuma-sacca-saññī yeva tasmiṃ samaye hoti.

puna	again	
ca	and	
paraṃ	further	
bhikkhu	m monk	
vūpasama	m (abl: after) suppression, cessation (of: gen)	[S vi-upa √śam]
ajjhatta	subjective, internal	
sampasādana	nt tranquillizing	[S sam-pra-√sad]
ceto	nt mind (gen sg)	
ekodibhāva	m concentration to one point	
a-vitakka	free from thought	
a-vicāra	free from investigation	
samādhi-ja	produced by concentration	
dutiya	second	

And again the monk leaves the analytic and investigating thought processes and enters and remains in the second meditation, a state of joy and happiness, born of concentration, free from analysis and investigation, an inner tranquillity and one-pointedness of the mind. The subtle but real awareness of joy and happiness, born of seclusion, which he formerly had, disappears. A subtle but real awareness of joy and happiness, born of concentration, arises at that time, and he becomes at that time subtly but truly aware of joy and happiness, born of concentration.

40. THE THIRD LEVEL OF CONCENTRATION (Digha Nikaya I 183)

Puna ca paraṃ bhikkhu pītiyā ca virāgā upekhako ca viharati sato ca sampajāno, sukhañ ca kāyena patisaṃvedeti yan taṃ ariyā ācikkhanti: "Upekhako satimā sukha-vihārī ti", tatiyajjhānaṃ upasampajja viharati. Tassa yā purimā samādhijaṃ pīti-sukhaṃ sukhuma-sacca-saññā sā nirujjhati. Upekhā-sukha-sukhuma-sacca-saññā tasmiṃ samaye hoti, upekhā-sukha-sukhuma-sacca-saññī yeva tasmiṃ samaye hoti.

pīti	f joy (gen sg)
virāga	m indifference, fading away (abl sg: after)
upekhaka	disinterested, neutral [S upa-√īkṣ, "onlooking"]
sata	mindful, conscious
sampajāna	attentive
kāya	m body (kayena instr "with his body" = "in his body")
patisaṃvedeti	feel, experience
yan taṃ (= yaṃ taṃ)	that which, "just so as"
ariya	noble
ācikkhati	tell, describe (pres ind 3 pl)
satimant	conscious, mindful (nom sg)
sukha-vihārin	dwelling in happiness (nom sg)
ti	marks end of quotation
tatiya	third
upekhā	f neutrality, equanimity

And again the monk leaves his feeling of joy and becomes neutral; he remains mindful and attentive, and he feels happiness in his body, just like the noble ones describe, "Neutral and mindful he is dwelling in happiness"; so he enters and remains in the third meditation. The subtle but real awareness of joy and happiness, born of concentration, which he formerly had, disappears. A subtle but real awareness of the happiness of equanimity arises at that time, and he becomes at that time subtly but truly aware of the happiness of equanimity.

Note

ariyā, "the noble ones": frequently used as a synonym for arahant, "worthy", "perfect", a person who has attained nirvana, the ultimate goal of Buddhism.

41. THE FOURTH LEVEL OF CONCENTRATION (Digha Nikaya I 183)

Puna ca paraṃ bhikkhu sukhassa ca pahānā dukkhassa ca pahānā pubb 'eva somanassa-domanassānaṃ atthagamā adukkhaṃ asukhaṃ upekhā-sati-pārisuddhiṃ catutthajjhānaṃ upasampajja viharati. Tassa yā purimā upekhā-sukha-sukhuma-sacca-saññā sā nirujjhati. Adukkha-m-asukha-sukhuma-sacca-saññā tasmiṃ samaye hoti, adukkha-m-asukha-sukhuma-sacca-saññī yeva tasmiṃ samaye hoti.

pahāna	nt leaving (abl sg)
pubba	former (here pubbe loc sg formerly, before)
somanassa	nt happiness, joy
domanassa	nt distress, dejectedness (gen pl)
atthagama	m "going (gama) home (attha)", disappearance
a-dukkha	free from discomfort
a-sukha	free from pleasure
sati	f mindfulness
pārisuddhi	f purity
catuttha	fourth

And again the monk leaves the feeling of pleasure and he leaves the feeling of discomfort; his former feelings of ease and distress disappear; he enters and remains in the fourth meditation, a pure state of equanimity and mindfulness free from pain and pleasure. The subtle but real awareness of the happiness of equanimity which he formerly had, disappears. A subtle but real awareness of freedom from pain and pleasure arises at that time, and he becomes at that time subtly but truly aware of freedom from pain and pleasure.

42. THE FIFTH, SIXTH AND SEVENTH LEVELS OF CONCENTRATION (Digha Nikaya I 183)

Puna ca paraṃ bhikkhu sabbaso rūpasaññānaṃ samatikkamā paṭigha-saññānaṃ atthagamā nānatta-saññānaṃ amanasi-kārā "ananto ākāso" ti ākāsānañcāyatanaṃ upasampajja viharati.

Puna ca paraṃ bhikkhu sabbaso ākāsānañcāyatanaṃ samatikkamma "anantaṃ viññāṇan" ti viññāṇānañcāyatanaṃ upasampajja viharati.

Puna ca paraṃ bhikkhu sabbaso viññāṇānañcāyatanaṃ samatikkamma "n'atthi kiñcīti" ākiñcaññāyatanaṃ upasampajja viharati.

sabbaso	altogether (abl to *sabba* all)
rūpa	nt form
saññā	f perception, consciousness, ideation (gen pl)
samatikkama	passing beyond (abl sg: "having passed beyond")
paṭigha	m, nt sensory reaction [S *prati-√ han*]
nānatta	m, nt diversity, manifoldness
a-manasikāra	m inattentiveness (abl sg; *a-* not, *kāra* making, *manas* mind)
an-anta	endless
ākāsa	m sky, space
ānañca	m infinity
āyatana	nt extent, sphere, dimension
samatikkamati	transcend (ger)
viññāṇa	nt consciousness
n'atthi	there is not
kiñci	nt something
iti	quotation mark
ākiñcañña	nt nothingness, emptiness

And again the monk altogether transcends the ideation of form; ideation depending on stimulation disappears; ideation of diversity is no longer noticed; thinking, "the space is endless" he enters and remains in the dimension of the infinity of space.

And again the monk altogether transcends the dimension of the infinity of space; thinking "consciousness is endless" he enters and remains in the dimension of the infinity of consciousness.

And again the monk altogether transcends the dimension of the infinity of consciousness; thinking, "nothing exists" he enters and remains in the dimension of nothingness.

Notes

rūpasaññānaṃ: saññā here refers to all types of mental representations of form, both perceived and remembered and imagined, in German "Vorstellung", we might say "ideation".

paṭigha-saññā is consciousness depending on external stimulation, i e perception; the monk no longer perceives anything.

These levels describe a certain psychological progress. The meditating monk starts from a rather normal conscious state made up of the usual stream of images, thoughts, perceptions, needs, feelings and emotions. On the first level of concentration, desires and unethical ideas are eliminated, on the second level thought processes disappear, then joy, and then feelings of pain and pleasure. When he enters the fifth level, he is neutral, i e free from needs and feelings, and begins to deal with his images and ideas: he tries to eliminate all details and differentiations; as a means to this end he tries to visualize the endless space. But this is still something external, and on the sixth level, it is replaced by something internal: the empty consciousness itself is visualized as endless. But this is still a visualization, an idea, however formless and vague, and the goal is not attained until even this is transcended. Two intermediary levels are needed in order to attain this: on the seventh level nothingness is visualized, freedom even from consciousness. But this is still an idea, the thinnest, vaguest, emptiest. It is on the verge of disappearing on the eighth level, and, if successful, the monk then finally enters into the final level, saññāvedayitanirodha, "the cessation of ideation and feeling". This is not a state of unconsciousness as is often maintained, neither of trance, but a state of absolute stillness and clarity, of undifferentiated holistic alertness. It is still not nirvana, only a means to attain nirvana.

For a description of these highest levels of concentration we turn to Anguttara Nikaya IV 448, where the Buddha relates how he himself attained to his goal with the help of these levels.

43. THE EIGHTH AND NINTH LEVELS OF CONCENTRATION
(Anguttara Nikaya IV 448)

So kho ahaṃ aparena samayena sabbaso nevasaññānāsaññāyatanaṃ samatikkamma saññāvedayitanirodhaṃ upasampajja viharāmi, paññāya ca me disvā āsavā parikkhayaṃ agamaṃsu.

Yato ca kho ahaṃ imā nava anupubbavihārasamāpattiyo evaṃ anulomapaṭilomaṃ samāpajjim pi vuṭṭhahim pi, athāhaṃ sadevake loke samārake sabrahmake sassamaṇabrāhmiṇiyā pajāya sadevamanussāya anuttaraṃ sammāsambodhiṃ abhisambuddho paccaññāsiṃ. Ñāṇañ ca pana me dassanaṃ udapādi: "akuppā me cetovimutti, ayam antimā jāti, n'atthi dāni punabbhavo" ti.

so ... ahaṃ	I myself
kho	indeed, then
apara	another, later
samaya	m time (instr sg)
aparena samayena	later on, afterwards
neva (= na eva) ... na	neither ... nor
a-saññā	f non-ideation
āyatana	nt extent, dimension
vedayita	p p nt what is felt, feeling
nirodha	m suppression, cessation
paññā	f understanding (instr sg)
me	instr to ahaṃ I
dassati	see, med-pass dissati see (for oneself), to which disvā ger "having seen (for myself)"
āsava	m influx, obsession
parikkhaya	m decay, disappearance
gacchati	go (agamaṃsu 3 pl aor)
parikkhayaṃ gacchati	"go to waste", i e disappear
yato	when
imā	(acc pl f) these
nava	nine
anupubba	successive, gradual
vihāra	m sojourn, state
samāpatti	f attainment (acc pl)
evaṃ	so, in this way
anuloma	"with the hair", i e in natural order, forward

paṭiloma	"against the hair", i e in reverse order, backward (here adv)
samāpajjati	attain (samāpajjiṃ: aor 1 sg)
pi ... pi	both ... and
vuṭṭhahati	emerge from (aor 1 sg) [S ud-√sthā]
atha	then
sa-deva-ka	together with (sa-) the gods (deva)
loka	m world (loc sg)
sa-māra-ka	together with (sa-) Māra
sa-brahma-ka	together with Brahma
sa-ssamaṇa-brāhmaṇī	together with recluses and brahmins (-ī adj suffix in f; here loc sg)
samaṇa	m recluse
brāhmaṇa	m member of the priest caste, brahmin
pajā	f offspring, mankind (loc sg)
sa-deva-manussa	together with gods (or kings) and men (loc sg)
an-uttara	"nothing higher", i e incomparable, unsurpassed
sammā	rightly, perfectly
sambodhi	f the highest insight (acc sg)
abhisambuddha	m one fully awakened, one who has completely understood (abhi, lit "over")
paṭijānāti	realize, understand (paccaññāsiṃ aor 1 sg)
ñāṇa	nt insight, understanding (nom sg)
ca pana	and
me	dat sg to ahaṃ I
dassana	nt seeing, insight
uppajjati	arise (udapādi 3 sg aor)
a-kuppa	immovable, safe
me	to me
ceto-vimutti	f liberation of mind
ayaṃ	this
antima	last, final
jāti	f birth
n'atthi	there is not
dāni	now
punabbhava	m new birth
ti	marks end of quotation

Thereafter I altogether transcended the dimension of neither-ideation-nor-non-ideation and entered and remained in the cessation of ideation and feeling. And when I got insight through understanding, the obsessions were expelled.

But when I had entered into and emerged from the attainment of these nine successive states, both forwards and backwards, then I completely understood and I attained the highest insight, which is unsurpassed in the world (with its gods, Māra and Brahma) and among mankind (with recluses, brahmins, gods and men). And the understanding and insight came to me, "Unshakeable is the liberation of my mind, this is my last birth, now there is no return".

Notes

nevasaññānāsaññāyatanaṃ, analyze: na- eva- saññā- na- asaññā- āyatanaṃ "the dimension which is neither ideation nor non-ideation".

Āsava is a term difficult to translate. The literal meaning is probably "influx". In Buddhist doctrine, it is used as a common term for four ideas which tend to fill the mind and prevent the attainment of nirvana: kāma, sensuality, bhava, rebirth, diṭṭhi, false doctrine, and avijjā, ignorance. These are usually mentioned as the last obstacles in the progress of the Buddhist aspirant. A tolerably good word in our language might be "obsessions".

imā nava anupubbavihārasamāpattiyo: "these nine successive-state--attainments"; we prefer to say "the attainment of these nine successive states".

deva means god, but in Indian literature it is also frequently used about kings.

Māra: the god of death and of temptation. Brahma: the supreme god according to Hindu mythology. Brahmin: a member of the highest caste in Hindu society, the caste of priests (although not every member was a priest).

It becomes clear from our text that nirvana is not identical with the highest level of concentration. It is just as essential that the āsavā are expelled and that full understanding is reached.

44. THE STATE OF EMPTINESS (Majjhima Nikaya III 293 f)

Eka-m-antaṃ nisinnaṃ kho āyasmantaṃ Sāriputtaṃ Bhagavā etad avoca: Vippasannāni kho te, Sāriputta, indriyāni parisuddho chavivaṇṇo pariyodāto. Katamena tvaṃ, Sāriputta, vihārena etarahi bahulaṃ viharasīti?

Suññatāvihārena kho ahaṃ, bhante, etarahi bahulaṃ viharāmīti.

Sādhu sādhu, Sāriputta. Mahāpurisavihārena kira tvaṃ, Sāriputta, etarahi bahulaṃ viharasi. Mahāpurisavihāro h'esa, Sāriputta, yadidaṃ suññatā.

ekamantaṃ	adv on one side, "at a respectful distance" (eka, one, anta m end)	
nisinna	sitting (p p to nisīdati sit)	
kho	indeed, then	
āyasmant	venerable (acc sg)	
Sāriputta	m one of the principle disciples of the Buddha	
bhagavant	lit fortunate; m master (nom sg)	
etad	nt this	
vatti	say (avoca 3 sg aor)	
vippasanna	pure, clear (nom pl nt)	[S vi-pra-√sīd]
te	your	
indriya	nt controlling power, sense function	
parisuddha	pure	
chavi	f skin	
vaṇṇa	m colour; chavi-vaṇṇa complexion	
pariyodāta	very clean	
katama	which?	
tvaṃ	you	
vihāra	m abode, state (instr sg)	
etarahi	now	
bahula	much (adv)	
viharati	stay, dwell (pres 2 sg)	
ti	marks end of quotation	
suññatā	f emptiness (suñña empty)	
bhante	voc sir!	
sādhu	good	
mahā-purisa	m great man	
kira	adv surely, truly	

hi	for
esa	this
yad idaṃ	namely

When the venerable Sariputta had taken his seat at a respectful distance, the Master said this to him, "Sariputta, your countenance is calm, and your complexion is pure and radiant. In which state do you now dwell much, Sariputta?"

"Sir, now I dwell much in the state of emptiness".

"Good, good, Sariputta! Surely you now dwell much in the state of great men. For this, Sariputta, is the state of great men, namely emptiness".

Notes

Indriya is a word for "trait" and "function", esp. "sensory function". But what the Buddha here noticed when looking at Sariputta was a special expression in his face: we therefore translate by "expression" or "countenance".

"Emptiness" is defined in different ways in the Buddhist literature. Here it may refer to the highest level of concentration, i e a state of fixed, undifferentiated, global awareness. The same question is namely found also in other contexts, where it is answered by referring to exercises in meditation. But another type of emptiness is also mentioned, namely freedom from obsessions (āsavā, cf text No. 43). In this case it is a synonym to nibbāna.

45. HOW TO MEET PERSECUTION AND DEATH (Majjhima Nikaya I 186)

Tañ-ce āvuso bhikkhuṃ pare aniṭṭhehi akantehi amanāpehi samudācaranti, pāṇisamphassena pi leḍḍusamphassena pi daṇḍasamphassena pi satthasamphassena pi, so evaṃ pajānāti: Tathābhūto kho ayaṃ kāyo yathābhūtasmiṃ kāye pāṇisamphassā pi kamanti, leḍḍusamphassā pi kamanti, daṇḍasamphassā pi kamanti, satthasamphassā pi kamanti. Vuttaṃ kho pan'etaṃ Bhagavatā Kakacūpamovāde: Ubhatodaṇḍakena ce pi bhikkhave kakacena corā ocarakā angamangāni okanteyyuṃ, tatra pi yo mano padoseyya na me so tena sāsanakaro ti. Āraddhaṃ kho pana me viriyaṃ bhavissati asallīnaṃ, upaṭṭhitā sati asammuṭṭhā, passaddho kāyo asāraddho, samāhitaṃ cittaṃ ekaggaṃ. Kāmaṃ dāni imasmiṃ kāye pāṇisamphassā pi kamantu, leḍḍusamphassā pi kamantu, daṇḍasamphassā pi kamantu, satthasamphassā pi kamantu, karīyati h'idaṃ buddhānaṃ sāsanan-ti.

sa	that (tañ- = taṃ, acc sg m)
ce	if
āvuso	(voc pl m) friends
bhikkhu	m monk
para	other (nom pl)
an-iṭṭha	not wanted, unpleasant (p p of icchati, instr pl)
a-kanta	not loved, undesirable (p p of kāmeti)
a-manāpa	not pleasant
sam-ud-ācarati	behave towards
pāṇi	m hand
samphassa	m contact, impact, "blow" (instr sg)
(a)pi ... (a)pi	both ... and
leḍḍu	m clod of earth
daṇḍa	m wooden stick
sattha	nt weapon, sword [S śastra]
so	he (nom sg m of sa)
evaṃ	so
pajānāti	know, understand
tathā-bhūta	become such (bhūta p p of bhavati, become)
kho	indeed
ayaṃ	demonstr pron this
kāya	body m
yathā-bhūta: tathā ... yathā,	such ... that

kamati	walk; affect (with loc). "This body has become such that blows from a hand affect such a body ..."
vutta	said (p p of vatti say)
pana	then, but, further
etaṃ	n this (esa m esā f)
bhagavant	adj fortunate; common epithet of the Buddha (instr): "Master"
kakaca	m saw
upamā	f parable
ovāda	m instruction (loc: "in the saw-parable instruction" i e, "in the instruction containing the parable of the saw")
ubhato	abl of ubho both; in compounds: twofold, double
daṇḍaka	m stick, handle; lit: "a small rod from both (ends)"; the compound is possessive
pi	even
bhikkhave	voc pl monks!
cora	m thief
ocaraka	m spy, bandit
anga	nt limb; anga-m-angāni limb by limb
okantati	cut off (opt 3 pl) [S ava-kṛntati]
tatra	there, in this
ya	rel pron who
mano	nt mind, internal sense
padoseti	causative verb derived from padosa m hatred, transl "make hateful", "fill with hate" [S pradveṣa]
na	not
me	enclitic gen of ahaṃ I
tena	nt, instr sg from sa that, he
sāsana	nt teaching
-kara	making, realizing, complying with
(i)ti	thus (marks end of statement)
āraddha	begun, firm; p p of ārabhati begin; viriyaṃ ārabhati make an effort
viriya	nt energy, vigour, effort
bhavati	become (fut)
a-sallīna	not sluggish, active, unshaken
upaṭṭhita	got ready, established; p p of upatiṭṭhāti put up
sati	f mindfulness, attention
a-sammuṭṭha	not confused; p p of mussati become bewildered [S √mṛṣ]
passaddha	composed, quieted; p p to passambhati, calm down

a-sāraddha	not excited
samāhita	composed, firm, attentive; p p to samādahati put together; cittaṃ samādahati concentrate the mind
citta	nt mind
ekagga	one-pointed, calm (eka one, agga nt top)
kāma	m nt pleasure, love; kāmaṃ acc as adv gladly
(i)dāni	adv now
ayaṃ	this (imasmiṃ m loc sg)
kamantu	imper 3 pl from kamati affect [S √kram]
karoti	do, make; 3 sg pres ind pass: karīyati "is being done"
hi	for
idaṃ	nt sg to ayaṃ this
buddha	awakened (gen pl)

Friends, if others behave in unpleasant, undesirable and nasty ways towards that monk, through blows from hands, clods of earth, sticks, or weapons, then he knows: "This body is such that blows from hands affect it, blows from clods of earth affect it, blows from sticks affect it and blows from weapons affect it. But exactly this was said by the Master in the instruction containing the parable of the saw, 'Monks, if thieves and bandits should cut off limb by limb with a two-handled saw, then whoever would fill his mind with hate would not follow my teaching thereby'. - Indeed, by me an unflinching effort shall be made, undisturbed mindfulness shall be established, the body shall be calm and relaxed, the mind shall be firm and one-pointed. Now let by all means blows from hands hit this body, let blows from clods of earth hit it, let blows from sticks hit it, let blows from weapons hit it; for this teaching of the Buddhas is being followed."

Notes

This text is taken from a discourse by Sariputta, one of the chief disciples of the Buddha. - "that monk": just before our text it is described how a monk makes it clear to himself that his body is impermanent and that there is nothing personal, nothing that really concerns him in it. This thought makes him happy and relaxed. - "The parable of the saw": the quotation is from M I 129. - The Buddhist way of meeting hostilities and physical pains is, then, meditation and a causal analysis of the origins of the pain.

anitthehi akantehi amanāpehi: "and" is frequently omitted; the words are to be understood as n pl "unpleasant ... things or ways"; it is the frequent idiomatic group iṭṭha kanta manāpa negated; the group means approximately "pleasant things".

46. A NUN TELLS HER STORY (Therigatha, verses 78-81)

Pariyuṭṭhitā kilesehi sukhasaññānuvattinī,
samaṃ cittassa nālabhiṃ rāgacittavasānugā.
Kisā paṇḍu vivaṇṇā ca satta vassāni cāri haṃ,
nāhaṃ divā vā rattiṃ vā sukhaṃ vindiṃ sudukkhitā.

Tato rajjuṃ gahetvāna pāvisiṃ vana-m-antaraṃ:
varaṃ me idha ubbandhaṃ yañ ca hīnaṃ pun'ācare.
Daḷhapāsaṃ karitvāna rukkhasākhāya bandhiya,
pakkhipiṃ pāsaṃ gīvāyaṃ, atha cittaṃ vimucci me.

pariyuṭṭhita	(p p to pari + uṭṭhahati rise) full of (+ instr, here nom sg f)	
kilesa	m impurity, defect, shortcoming (instr pl)	[S kleśa]
sukha	pleasant	
saññā	f perception, experience	
anuvattin	following, hunting (nom sg f)	
sama	m calmness	[S √śam]
citta	nt mind (gen sg)	
na	not	
labhati	receive, acquire (alabhiṃ aor 1 sg)	
rāga	m passion, desire; rāga-citta a mind full of desire	
vasa	m, nt power, influence	[S vaśa]
anuga	following, being under the influence of	
vasānuga	in the power of	
kisa	lean, emaciated	[S kṛśa]
paṇḍu	pale	
vivaṇṇa	colourless	
ca	and	
satta	seven	[S sapta]
vassa	nt year (acc pl)	[S varṣa]
carati	move, live (cāri aor 1 sg)	
ahaṃ	I	
na ... vā ... vā	neither ... nor	
divā	adv by day	
rattiṃ	adv by night	

vindati	find (vindiṃ aor 1 sg)
su-dukkhita	very unhappy (nom f sg)
tato	then
rajju	f rope (acc sg)
gaṇhati	grasp, take (gahetvāna ger, "having taken")
pavisati	enter (pāvisiṃ aor 1 sg)
vana	nt forest
antara	nt inside ("to the inside of the forest" = into the forest)
vara	excellent
varaṃ (nt)... yaṃ	(it is) better ... than
me	acc me
idha	here
ubbandhati	hang up, strangle (pres p)
yañ ca (+ opt)	than that ...
hīna	low, miserable
puna	again
ācarati	practice, indulge in (ācare opt 1 sg)
daḷha	strong [S dṛdha]
pāsa	m snare, noose [S pāśa]
karoti	make (karitvāna ger, "having made")
rukkha	m tree [S vṛkṣa]
sākhā	f branch (loc sg) [S śākhā]
bandhati	bind (bandhiya ger, "having bound")
pakkhipati	throw into, place around (pakkhipiṃ aor 1 sg)
gīvā	f neck (loc sg) [S grīvā]
atha	then
vimuccati (pass to vi-muñcati liberate)	become free (aor 3 sg pass)
me	gen "my", or dat "for me"

Full of defects and hunting for happiness, I did not win calmness of mind, because I was in the power of my sensual mind.
Emaciated, pale and colourless I lived for seven years. Very unhappy, I could not find happiness, neither by day nor by night.
Then I took a rope and went deep into the forest, "It is better that I hang myself here than that I again pursue (= continue) the misery".
When I had made a strong noose and bound it to a branch of a tree, I placed it around my neck: then my mind became free.

Note

This text is quoted from Therigatha, "Psalms of the Nuns", which consists of a collection of poems attributed to different nuns from the earliest order (sangha). There is also a "Psalms of the Monks" (Theragatha), see texts No. s 48–49.

"My mind became free": another expression for the attainment of nirvana. The text tells us something about the nature of nirvana: it will not always come as a natural result of a planfully completed program, as we have seen in earlier quotations, but it may come, even at unexpected moments, as a sudden experience of clarity and new meaning.

47. THE BUDDHA RELATES HOW HE ATTAINED NIRVANA
(Majjhima Nikaya I 167)

Attanā sankilesadhammo samāno sankilesadhamme ādīnavaṃ viditvā asankiliṭṭhaṃ anuttaraṃ yogakkhemaṃ nibbānaṃ pariyesamāno asankiliṭṭhaṃ anuttaraṃ yogakkhemaṃ nibbānaṃ ajjhagamaṃ. Ñāṇañ-ca pana me dassanaṃ udapādi: Akuppā me vimutti, ayaṃ antimā jāti, n'atthi dāni punabbhavo 'ti.

attā	m self (instr sg)
sankilesa	m impurity
dhamma	m nature
samāna	being (pres p to atthi, is)
ādīnava	m danger, disadvantage (acc sg)
vindati	find, understand (viditvā ger having understood)
a-sankiliṭṭha	unstained
an-uttara	unsurpassed
yogakkhema	nt rest (khema) from work (yoga m), peace from bondage [S kṣema]
nibbāna	nt, nirvana, the goal of Buddhism
pariyesati	seek (pres p) [S pari-ā-√iṣ]
adhigacchati	go to, attain (aor 1 sg)
ñāṇa	nt understanding, knowledge
ca	and
pana	further, then
me	to me
dassana	nt insight
uppajjati	arise (udapādi aor 3 sg)
akuppa	unshakeable, steadfast (nom sg f)
me	my
vimutti	f release, liberation
ayaṃ	m and f this
antima	last, final
jāti	f birth
na atthi	there is not
dāni	adv now
punabbhava	m renewed existence
ti	marks end of quotation

Being impure by nature, through my own doing, I understood the danger in being impure. Seeking the stainless, incomparable peace: nirvana, I attained the stainless, incomparable peace: nirvana. And then the knowledge and insight came to me: "Unshakeable is my release, this is my last birth, now there is no coming back".

Notes

attanā, "because of the self", "by my own doing".

sankilesa-dhamma possessive compound: "having impurity-nature", "being impure by nature"; sankilesa-dhamme loc sg, "in impurity-nature", i e in being impure by nature.

Our quotation is only a small part of a larger context, where exactly the same formulation is used about "liability to birth", "liability to ageing", "liability to decay", "liability to dying" etc.

The exact meaning of yoga is uncertain. From a linguistic point of view it is quite possible to translate "peace through yoga exercises", but in Buddhist literature the word yoga is not used for meditation.

The text proves that the Buddha attained nirvana in the moment of the so-called "enlightenment". This is important for the definition of the word nirvana. We are never told that he again left or emerged from nirvana. So it probably refers to a permanent state. Cf the following quotations.

48. NIRVANA (Theragatha, verse 79)

Sabbo rāgo pahīno me
sabbo doso samūhato,
sabbo me vigato moho;
sītibhūto 'smi nibbuto.

sabba	all, every
rāga	m desire, passion
pahīna	p p abandoned (from pajahati leave)
me	from me, by me
dosa	m hate
samūhata	p p removed (from samūhanati remove)
vigata	p p gone away, ceased (from vigacchati depart)
moha	m illusion
sīta	cool [S śīta]
bhūta	p p become (to hoti is, becomes)
sītibhūta	cool, calm
asmi	I am
nibbuta	extinguished (of fire), having attained nibbāna

All desire has been abandoned by me.
All hate is removed.
All illusion has disappeared from me.
I am cool and have attained nirvana.

Note

The state called nirvana has got its name from a simile: a fire that is extinguished. Nirvana means extinction. When the internal fire (the desire to live, the aggressiveness, the illusion) has been extinguished, one becomes "cool", i e neutral and balanced.

49. HAPPINESS (Theragatha, verse 227)

Susukhaṃ vata nibbānaṃ
sammāsambuddhadesitaṃ,
asokaṃ virajaṃ khemaṃ
yattha dukkhaṃ nirujjhati.

susukha	very pleasant; nt highest happiness
vata	certainly
sammā	rightly, perfectly
sambuddha	having thoroughly understood
desita	p p taught (to deseti teach)
a-soka	free from sorrow
viraja	stainless
khema	nt peace, security
yattha	where
dukkha	nt suffering
nirujjhati	be dissolved (pass to nirundhati destroy)

The highest happiness is indeed nirvana,
which has been taught by him
who has perfectly understood,
the sorrow-less, stainless security
where suffering is dissolved.

50. NIRVANA IS WITHIN REACH (Therigatha, verses 511-513)

Ajaramhi vijjamāne kin tava kāmehi ye sujarā?
Maraṇabyādhigahitā sabbā sabbattha jātiyo.
Idam ajaram idam amaraṃ
idam a-jarā-maraṇa-padam asokaṃ,
asapattam asambādhaṃ akhalitam
abhayaṃ nirupatāpaṃ.
Adhigatam idaṃ bahūhi amataṃ
ajjāpi ca labhanīyam idaṃ.

a-jara	nt freedom from old age (loc sg)	
vindati	find (vijjamāne loc sg pres p pass)	
kiṃ	what?	
tava	(dat of tvaṃ) for you	
kāma	m or nt, pleasure	
ya	rel pron, who, which (nom pl)	
sujara	quickly ageing (nom pl)	
maraṇa	nt death	
byādhi	m illness	[S vyādhi]
gahita	p p seized (from gaṇhāti grasp)	
sabba	all	
sabbattha	everywhere	
jāti	f birth, life (nom pl)	
idaṃ	nt this	
a-mara	free from death	
jarā	f old age	
pada	nt way, characteristic, "state"	
a-soka	free from sorrow	
a-sapatta	without enmity	
a-sambādha	not crowded, unobstructed	
a-khalita	undisturbed	
a-bhaya	without fear	
nir-upatāpa	free from pain	
adhigata	p p attained (to adhigacchati go to)	
bahu	much, many (instr pl: by many)	
a-mata	free from death (mata p p of marati die)	
ajja	today	[S adya]
api	even	
ca	and	
labhanīya	f p p attainable (to labhati attain)	

When freedom from old age is found, what use have you for pleasures that quickly grow old? All lives, everywhere, are caught by death and illness. This is freedom from old age, this is freedom from death, this is the state without old age and death, without sorrow, without enmity, without obstacle, without disturbance, without fear, without pain. This state without death has been attained by many: even today it may be attained.

Notes

Ajaramhi vijjamāne: absolute loc, "when freedom from old age is found".

The idea "What is the use of" is expressed by kiṃ + dat of the person + instr of the thing. Here: "What use have you for pleasures?"

amara does not imply that a person who has attained nirvana shall not die physically. It means rather a state without rebirth. A man who is not reborn cannot again grow old and die. "Immortality" is therefore not a good translation.

51. THE UNBORN (Udana, p 80)

Atthi, bhikkhave, ajātaṃ abhūtaṃ akataṃ asankhataṃ, no ce taṃ, bhikkhave, abhavissa ajātaṃ abhūtaṃ akataṃ asankhataṃ, na yidha jātassa bhūtassa katassa sankhatassa nissaraṇaṃ paññāyetha. Yasmā ca kho, bhikkhave, atthi ajātaṃ abhūtaṃ akataṃ asankhataṃ, tasmā jātassa bhūtassa katassa sankhatassa nissaraṇaṃ paññāyatī 'ti.

atthi	there is
bhikkhu	m monk (voc pl)
a-jāta	not born (p p to janati produce, nt nom sg)
a-bhūta	not become (p p to bhavati become)
a-kata	not made (p p to karoti make)
a-sankhata	not put together (p p to sankharoti, put together, create)
no	but not, and not
ce	if
taṃ	that
bhavati	become, be (abhavissa cond 3 sg "there had been")
na	not
(y)idha	here
jāta	born (gen sg)
bhūta	become
kata	made
sankhata	compound
nissaraṇa	nt escape (+ gen = from)
paññāyati	be known (pass to pajānāti understand; paññāyetha opt med 3 sg "would be known")
yasmā	because, since (rel pron abl sg)
ca	and
kho	indeed
tasmā	therefore (pron sa, he, that, abl sg)
ti	marks end of quotation

Monks, there is something that is not born, not become, not made, not compound. For, monks, if there had not been this which is not born, not become, not made, not compound, then an escape from the born, the become, the made, the compound, would not be known here. But, monks, since there is something not born, not become, not made, not compound, therefore an escape from the born, the become, the made, the compound is known.

Note

This text is very frequently quoted as proving that nirvana is not only a psychological state of the human personality but also something transcendent, a metaphysical entity. It is, however, doubtful whether this idea has to be implied, since the adjectives have no noun. What is "not born, not become" etc? We need not necessarily imply a word meaning "element" or "reality". A word meaning "state" would be in better agreement with the general tendency of early Buddhism to speak about human problems rather than metaphysics. The translation would then be "a state without birth, without becoming, without production and without compounding". The text is then interpreted as pointing out that nirvana is a state without rebirth and without change, just as so many other texts do. A more detailed discussion of the concept nirvana is found in the book "The Psychology of Nirvana" by the present writer (Allen and Unwin, London, 1969).

52. NIRVANA AND DEATH (Sutta Nipata, verses 1074, 1076)

Accī yathā vātavegena khitto
atthaṃ paleti na upeti sankhaṃ,
evaṃ munī nāmakāyā vimutto
atthaṃ paleti na upeti sankhaṃ.

Atthan gatassa na pamāṇam atthi
yena naṃ vajju, taṃ tassa n'atthi
sabbesu dhammesu samūhatesu
samūhatā vādapathā pi sabbe.

accī	f ray of light, flame
yathā	just as
vāta	m wind
vega	m force, speed (instr sg)
khitta	p p thrown, blown out (to khipati throw)
attha	nt home
atthaṃ paleti	go to rest, disappear
na	not
sankhā	f calculation, definition
upeti	go to
sankhaṃ na upeti	cannot be defined
evaṃ	so
muni	m (-ī for metric reasons) sage
nāma	nt name
kāya	m body (abl sg)
vimutta	freed (p p to vimuñcati release)
atthan gata	having gone to rest (dat sg)
pamāṇa	nt measure, definition, description
atthi	there is
yena	through which (rel pron instr sg)
naṃ	him (acc sg)
vadati	say, tell (vajju opt 3 sg, "one could describe")
taṃ	nt that
tassa	(dat sg of so) for him
na atthi	is not
sabba	all (loc pl)
dhamma	m idea, image
samūhata	p p removed (to samūhanati remove)

vāda	m speech, attribute
patha	m way
vāda-patha	way of speech, sign of recognition
(a)pi	even

Like a flame that has been blown out by a strong wind, goes to rest and cannot be defined, just so the sage who is freed from name and body, goes to rest and cannot be defined.

For him who has gone to rest there is no measure by means of which one could describe him; that is not for him. When all ideas have gone, all signs of recognition have also gone.

Notes

muni is here used in the same sense as arahant, i e "perfect", one who has attained nirvana.

nāma-kāya "name and body" probably means mind and body, the psychological and physical aspects of personality.

sabbesu dhammesu samūhatesu is an absolute loc: "when all ideas are gone".

The first stanza is given as an answer to the question whether a consciousness will develop (bhavetha viññāṇaṃ) for him who has attained the goal. The problem is, simply, what will happen to the arahant when he dies. The answer is not that he is annihilated but that he will exist in some indefinable form, just as a fire that is extinguished is not annihilated according to the Indian view but has withdrawn into the matter and exists in some unknown form.

"ideas": we should remember that the difference between an arahant and other people at the moment of death concerns consciousness (viññāṇa). Usually this is filled with desires and ideas (dhammā): by means of the energy load in these, a new individual is produced. But in the arahant, consciousness is "calm", "stilled", which means that it is undifferentiated and free from single desires and ideas. But what is undifferentiated cannot be described: there are no attributes, no characteristics.

SUMMARY OF GRAMMAR

G 1. Pali is not a difficult language. The grammar is rich in inflections, but not so rich as many other languages: and inflections are also helpful. But to the beginner it may make a "strange" and somewhat heavy impression, the reason being mainly syntactical differences between his own language and Pali. A good English translation must often be constructed in a radically different way. Let us point out a few such differences.

a) There are no definite or indefinite articles in Pali, although a demonstrative pronoun and the numeral for "one" occasionally may be used for these purposes.

b) The personal pronouns are not used as subjects to verbs except when stressed, since the person is indicated by means of endings.

c) The copula (i e different forms of "be") is usually omitted. We say, for instance, "this is suffering", but in Pali this would be idaṃ dukkhaṃ, without atthi. In text No. 1 we read Satthā no garu, "our teacher is venerable", but the text has no atthi.

d) The verb is usually placed at the end of the sentence.

e) Pali frequently prefers a noun where we would find a verb more suitable. See, for instance, text No. 4 where the whole of the second sentence consists of a number of nouns. In natural English we would use verbs. In No. 42 we find a noun samatikkamā in ablative, meaning "after the transcending of". Similar examples will be found, e g in No. 35 (anuppādāya) and No. 39 (vūpasamā). In English either a temporal clause or a coordinated main clause is used.

f) A clear distinction is often not made between different classes of words and between different grammatical functions. Nouns may sometimes be used as adjectives, cases may be given untypical functions in a sentence, and it sometimes has to be concluded from the context whether a certain verb-form is to be given active or passiv meaning.

g) Subordinate clauses are not so common in Pali. Subordination is more often expressed by means of absolute expressions, compounds and participles.

h) Compounds are very common in Pali. They may be very complex and may be given functions in the sentence that are impossible in English. They have to be studied carefully. See G 8.

i) Pali frequently prefers negative expressions although the meaning is positive, e g a-vippaṭisāra, "free from bad conscience", avyāpāda, "non-violence" = "kindness", avihiṃsā, "freedom from cruelty" = "compassion".

j) In Pali some types of passive expressions are very common, especially past participles and passive future participles.

k) In English, the words 'and' and 'if' always are placed first in a sentence, while in Pali their equivalents ca and ce are always placed as second words, e g in No. 2 Katamañ ca "And what". Several other words have the same enclitic position in the sentence: vā "or", hi "because", (a)pi "even".

l) In conversations the speaker usually appeals to the listener in every sentence by means of a vocative, e g bhikkhave, "monks!"

m) The rules of punctuation are different in Pali and English. In most Pali editions, there are very few commas. In Pali manuscripts, direct speech and other quotations are marked only by a ti after the last word, but in some European editions, quotation marks are added (in our texts, there are examples of both). Pali has a word ca for "and", but this is frequently omitted and the coordination has to be inferred from the context. See, e g, No. 43: loke....pajāya "in the world .... and among mankind". Sometimes it need not be translated, since it merely marks a connection with what has been said before.

G 2. Nouns and Adjectives

Pali has the following cases:

a) Nominative, which is the case of the subject and its attributes. Example (Text No. 1): Api nu tumhe (nom pl) ··· evaṃ jānantā (nom pl) ··· vadeyyātha "Would you perhaps, knowing this ··· speak so?" The predicate is also nominative, if its head-word is nominative: Satthā no garu (nom) "Our teacher is venerable" (No. 1).

b) Accusative is the case of the direct object: nīlakaṃ sañjānāti (No. 11) "he perceives blue". The accusative can further be used as an adverb, especially to express direction and extension (in time or space): satta vassāni (No. 46) "during seven years", rattiṃ (No. 46) "by night". The goal of a motion is also expressed by means of the accusative case: parikkhayaṃ agamaṃsu (No. 43) "they went to their destruction".

c) Dative is the case of the indirect object, for instance, the person to whom something is given. Generally, the dative is used to express the person who has the advantage of some action.
Examples: tassa me (dat) Tathāgato ··· dhammaṃ desesi (No. 26) "The Buddha .... taught me the doctrine"; taṃ tassa n'atthi (No. 52) "that is not for him"; me dassanaṃ udapādi (No. 43) "the insight came to me". Further, the intention or purpose may be expressed by the dative: ··· akusalānaṃ dhammānaṃ pahānāya (dat) chandaṃ janeti (No. 35) "he makes a resolution in order to expell inappropriate processes". Here pahāna is a verbal noun corresponding to our "rejection". It is put in the dative case in order to express the purpose; we use a prepositional expression "in order to".

The dative case is often difficult to distinguish from genitive, since the form is usually the same. The meanings are also often quite close to each other: cittaṃ vimucci me (No. 46) "my mind was liberated" (gen), or "the mind was liberated for me".

It should also be pointed out that Pali has no equivalent to our verb "have". The idea may be expressed in many ways, e g atthi + dat or gen "there is (to me)". Ex. mama dve puttā santi "I have two sons".

d) By means of the genitive case the idea of possession is expressed. Example: buddhānaṃ sāsanaṃ (No. 45) "the teaching of the Buddhas", samaṃ cittassa (No. 46) "calmness of the mind". This idea is, however, as vaguely conceived as in the English expressions with "of", e g viññāṇassa nirodha (No. 16), "the stopping of consciousness", tiṇṇaṃ sangati (No. 19), "the combination of the three", pītiyā virāgā (No. 40) "after the disappearance of joy", jātassa ··· nissaraṇaṃ (No. 51) "escape from the born". The genitive is the most common case for expressing relations between nouns.

e) The instrumental case indicates the instrument or the cause: paññāya ··· disvā (No. 43) "when I got insight through understanding", attanā (No. 47) "through my own doing", pariyuṭṭhitā kilesehi (No. 46) "full of defects". It is used to express companionship or possession:

saddhāya samannāgato (No. 24), "endowed with faith". It is also the case of the agent in passive expressions: diṭṭhigataṃ te (No. 8) "you have gone to false theory"; upanītā ... me (instr, agent) ... iminā ... dhammena (instr, the instrument) ... veditabbena viññūhi (instr, agent) (No. 1), "you have been instructed by me ... through the doctrine ... that can be understood by the intelligent".

f) The ablative case is used to express movement away from something and release from something. nāmakāyā vimutto (No. 52), "freed from name and body", sukhāya vedanāya rāgānusayo pahātabbo (No. 10) "a tendency to desire is to be eliminated from the pleasant feeling"; musāvādā paṭivirato (No. 30) "abstaining from false speech". The ablative can also express what has happened before something: rūpa-saññānaṃ samatikkamā (No. 42) "after transcending the idea of form". The idea "in terms of", "as" is expressed by means of the ablative: te dhamme aniccato ... samanupassati (No. 9) "he regards these things as impermanent". Adverbial expressions in the ablative are frequently found: sabbaso (No. 42), "altogether", tasmā (No. 11), "therefore".

g) The locative case indicates time and place: khette (No. 20) "in the field", gīvāyaṃ (No. 46) "round the neck", tasmiṃ samaye (No. 39), "at that time". A way to express subordinate clauses, especially temporal and causal clauses, is the so-called absolute locative. In this construction, both the subject and the verb take the locative case: ajaramhi vijjamāne (No. 50) "when freedom from old age is found", khandhesu santesu (No. 8), "when the factors are present". The subject may be omitted if it is self-evident in the context: gate (No. 36) "when he goes".

h) The vocative case is used when somebody is addressed: bhikkhave, "monks!"

G 3. The Pali adjectives and nouns are inflected in different ways depending on the final sound of the stem. In order to inflect a Pali word correctly we have to know the stem; therefore, this is given in dictionaries and vocabularies rather than the nominative.

In the following we illustrate the inflections of the most common stem-types.

a) Masculine and neuter stems ending in -a and feminine stems in -ā (sacca, "true")

Singular

	Masc	Neut	Fem
Nom	sacco	saccaṃ	saccā
Voc	sacca	saccaṃ	sacce
Acc	saccaṃ	saccaṃ	saccaṃ
Instr	saccena saccā	= Masc	saccāya
Dat	saccassa saccāya	= Masc	saccāya
Gen	saccassa	= Masc	saccāya
Abl	saccā saccasmā saccamhā saccato	= Masc	saccāya
Loc	sacce saccasmiṃ saccamhi	= Masc	saccāya saccāyaṃ

Plural

	Masc	Neut	Fem
Nom	saccā	saccāni saccā	saccā saccāyo
Voc	saccā	saccāni saccā	saccā saccāyo
Acc	sacce	saccāni saccā	saccā saccāyo
Instr	saccehi	= Masc	saccāhi
Abl	saccehi	= Masc	saccāhi
Dat	saccānaṃ	= Masc	saccānaṃ
Gen	saccānaṃ	= Masc	saccānaṃ
Loc	saccesu	= Masc	saccāsu

b) Masculine stems in -u and -i are inflected in the same way, except for the vowel itself. We illustrate by showing the forms of bhikkhu "monk"

	Singular	Plural
Nom	bhikkhu	bhikkhū, bhikkhavo
Voc	bhikkhu	bhikkhave
Acc	bhikkhuṃ	bhikkhū, bhikkhavo
Instr	bhikkhunā	bhikkhūhi
Abl	bhikkhusmā, bhikkhumhā bhikkhunā, bhikkhuto	bhikkhūhi
Dat	bhikkhuno, bhikkhussa	bhikkhūnaṃ
Gen	bhikkhuno, bhikkhussa	bhikkhūnaṃ
Loc	bhikkhumhi	bhikkhūsu

c) Feminine stems ending in -i and -u: jāti, "birth"

	Singular	Plural
Nom	jāti	jātiyo, jātī
Voc	jāti	jātiyo, jātī
Acc	jātiṃ	jātiyo, jātī
Instr	jātiyā	jātīhi
Dat	jātiyā	jātīnaṃ
Gen	jātiyā	jātīnaṃ
Abl	jātiyā	jātīhi
Loc	jātiyā, jātiyaṃ	jātīsu

d) Stems in -r. Example: satthar, m "teacher".

	Singular	Plural
Nom	satthā	satthāro
Voc	sattha, satthe, satthā	satthāro
Acc	satthāraṃ	satthāro

Instr	satthara, satthārā, satthunā	satthūhi, satthārehi
Dat	satthu, satthuno, satthussa	satthūnaṃ, satthārānaṃ
Gen	satthu, satthuno, satthussa	satthūnaṃ, satthārānaṃ
Abl	satthara, satthārā	satthūhi, satthārehi
Loc	satthari	satthūsu, satthāresu

e) Stems ending in -in: vādin, "saying" (in masc a stem vādi with the endings of bhikkhu is also found, G 3 b)

	Masc sg	Masc pl	Fem sg	Fem pl
Nom	vādī	vādino	vādinī	vādinī
Voc	vādi	vādino	vādini	vādinī
Acc	vādinaṃ	vādino	vādiniṃ	vādinī
Instr	vādinā	vādīhi	vādiniyā	vādinīhi
Abl	vādinā	vādīhi	vādiniyā	vādinīhi
Dat	vādino	vādīnaṃ	vādiniyā	vādinīnaṃ
Gen	vādino	vādīnaṃ	vādiniyā	vādinīnaṃ
Loc	vādini	vādīsu	{ vādiniyā vādiniyaṃ	vādinīsu

f) Stems ending in -nt: gacchant "going", satimant "mindful"

	Sing		Plur	
Nom	gacchaṃ	satimā	gacchanto	satimanto
Voc	gacchaṃ	satimā	gacchanto	satimanto
Acc	gacchantaṃ	satimantaṃ	gacchanto	satimanto
Instr	gacchatā	satimatā	gacchantehi	satimantehi
Abl	gacchatā	satimatā	gacchantehi	satimantehi
Dat	gacchato	satimato	gacchataṃ	satimataṃ
Gen	gacchato	satimato	gacchataṃ	satimataṃ
Loc	gacchati	satimati	gacchantesu	satimantesu

Present participles are usually inflected like gacchant, but sometimes an -a is added to the stem and the inflection follows the -a-stems (e g gacchanto, No. 36).

g) Neutral stems in -as. Ex. manas "mind", "internal sense" (we find also the form mana, inflected like stems in -a, e g in text No. 14)

	Sing	Plur
Nom, Voc, Acc	mano	
Instr	manasā	Like a-stems
Dat, Gen	manaso	
Loc	manasi	

h) Stems ending in -an: rājan m "king", attan m "self"

	Sing	Plur
Nom	rājā	rājāno
Voc	rājā, rāja	rājāno
Acc	rājānaṃ	rājāno
Instr	rājinā, raññā	rājūhi
Abl	raññā, rājato	rājūhi
Dat	rañño, rājino	raññaṃ, rājūnaṃ
Gen	rañño, rājino	raññaṃ, rājūnaṃ
Loc	rājini	rājāsu
Nom	attā	attāno
Voc	attā, atta	attāno
Acc	attānaṃ	attāno
Instr	attanā	attanehi, attehi
Abl	attanā	attanehi, attehi
Dat	attano	attānaṃ
Gen	attano	attānaṃ
Loc	attani	attanesu

G 4. Pronouns

a) ahaṃ "I"

	Singular	Plural
Nom	ahaṃ "I"	mayaṃ "we"
Acc	maṃ	amhe, asme, no
Instr	mayā, me	amhehi, no
Abl	mayā	amhehi
Dat	mayhaṃ, mama, me	amhākaṃ, asmākaṃ, no
Gen	mayhaṃ, mama, me	amhākaṃ, asmākaṃ, no
Loc	mayi	amhesu

b) tvaṃ "you"

Nom	tvaṃ, tuvaṃ "you"	tumhe, "you"
Acc	taṃ, tvaṃ, tuvaṃ	tumhe, tumhākaṃ, vo
Instr	tayā, tvayā, te	tumhehi, vo
Abl	tayā, tvayā	tumhehi
Dat	tuyhaṃ, tava, te	tumhākaṃ, vo
Gen	tuyhaṃ, tava, te	tumhākaṃ, vo
Loc	tayi, tvayi	tumhesu

c) The demonstrative pronoun so, "he", "it", "this"

Singular

	Masc	Neut	Fem
Nom	so	taṃ, tad	sā
Acc	taṃ	taṃ, tad	taṃ
Instr	tena	= Masc	tāya
Abl	tamhā, tasmā	= Masc	tāya
Dat	tassa	= Masc	tassā, tissā, tāya
Gen	tassa	= Masc	tassā, tissā, tāya
Loc	tamhi, tasmiṃ	= Masc	tassaṃ, tissaṃ / tāsaṃ, tāyaṃ

Plural

	Masc	Neut	Fem
Nom	te	tāni	tā, tāyo
Acc	te	tāni	tā, tāyo
Instr	tehi	= Masc	tāhi
Abl	tehi	= Masc	tāhi
Dat	tesaṃ	= Masc	tāsaṃ
Gen	tesaṃ	= Masc	tāsaṃ
Loc	tesu	= Masc	tāsu

d) The demonstrative pronoun ayaṃ "this"

Singular

	Masc	Neut	Fem
Nom	ayaṃ	idaṃ, imaṃ	ayaṃ
Acc	imaṃ	idaṃ, imaṃ	imaṃ
Instr	iminā, anena	= Masc	imāya
Abl	imasmā, imamhā asmā	= Masc	imāya
Dat	imassa, assa	= Masc	imissā, imāya, assā
Gen	imassa, assa	= Masc	imissā, imāya, assā
Loc	imasmiṃ, imamhi, asmiṃ	= Masc	imissaṃ, imissā imāyaṃ, assaṃ

Plural

	Masc	Neut	Fem
Nom	ime	imāni	imā, imāyo
Acc	ime	imāni	imā, imāyo
Instr	imehi	= Masc	imāhi
Abl	imehi	= Masc	imāhi
Dat	imesaṃ, esaṃ	= Masc	imāsaṃ, āsaṃ
Gen	imesaṃ, esaṃ	= Masc	imāsaṃ, āsaṃ
Loc	imesu, esu	= Masc	imāsu

e) The relative pronoun ya, "who", "which"

Singular

	Masc	Neut	Fem
Nom	yo	yaṃ, yad	yā
Acc	yaṃ	yaṃ, yad	yaṃ
Instr	yena	= Masc	yāya
Abl	yasmā, yamhā	= Masc	yāya
Dat	yassa	= Masc	yassā, yāya
Gen	yassa	= Masc	yassā, yāya
Loc	yasmiṃ, yamhi	= Masc	yassaṃ, yāyaṃ

Plural

	Masc	Neut	Fem
Nom	ye	yāni	yā, yāyo
Acc	ye	yāni	yā, yāyo
Instr	yehi	= Masc	yāhi
Abl	yehi	= Masc	yāhi
Dat	yesaṃ	= Masc	yāsaṃ
Gen	yesaṃ	= Masc	yāsaṃ
Loc	yesu	= Masc	yāsu

f) The interrogative pronoun ka "who ?" "what?"

Singular

	Masc	Neut	Fem
Nom	ko	kiṃ	kā
Acc	kaṃ	kiṃ	kaṃ
Instr	kena	= Masc	kāya
Abl	kasmā, kismā	= Masc	kāya
Dat	kassa, kissa	= Masc	kassā, kāya
Gen	kassa, kissa	= Masc	kassā, kāya
Loc	kamhi, kimhi kismiṃ, kasmiṃ	= Masc	kassaṃ, kāyaṃ

Plural

	Masc	Neut	Fem
Nom	ke	kāni	kā
Acc	ke	kāni	kā
Instr	kehi	= Masc	kāhi
Abl	kehi		kāhi
Dat	kesaṃ		kāsaṃ
Gen	kesaṃ		kāsaṃ
Loc	kesu		kāsu

G 5. The Verb

The verb has finite and infinite forms. The finite forms are conjugated, i e take different terminations for the different persons. The infinite forms are inflected like adjectives or not inflected at all.

Pali has active and passive voice but in addition a "middle" voice (usually called medium) which originally was used to express action in the interest of the subject, e g "I work for myself", reflexive action, "I help myself" or reciprocal action, "we help each other". The medium forms are not frequent in Pali. The few forms occurring in the texts are specially pointed out in the vocabularies. The meaning can usually not be distinguished from the active.

The tenses are formed by using different stems. Most common is the present stem which is used to express present time (i e gaccha-ti "he goes", "he is going"). From this, a future stem and a passive stem are constructed by adding suffixes (-iss- and -ya-, respectively). Aorist, which is used to express past tense, and the passive past participle are formed from special stems.

In addition to the ordinary indicative mood, which just states a fact, Pali has an imperative, which expresses a command and can be used for all persons, and an optative which expresses a wish. There is also a conditional mood used in conditional clauses, i e clauses beginning with "if" (Pali ce).

In the following, the most common inflections will be exemplified. In order to facilitate a quick orientation among all the different verb forms, we have collected the principle parts of a few very common verbs in the table on the next page.

G 6. Finite Forms

a) Present indicative active and passive

	Active		Passive	
Sg 1	labhāmi	"I receive"	labbhāmi	"I am received"
2	labhasi	"you receive"	labbhasi	"you are received"
3	labhati	"he, she receives"	labbhati	"he, she is received"
Pl 1	labhāma	"we receive"	labbhāma	"we are received"
2	labhatha	"you receive"	labbhatha	"you are received"
3	labhanti	"they receive"	labbhanti	"they are received"

Note. The present is also sometimes used as a narrative tense: "I received" etc.

Pres med is conjugated as follows:

Sg 1	labhe
2	labhase
3	labhate
Pl 1	labhamhe
2	labhavhe
3	labhante, labhare

b) Imperative

Sg 1	labhāmi	"may I receive"
2	labha, labhāhi	"receive!"
3	labhatu	"may he receive"
Pl 1	labhāma	"may we receive"
2	labhatha	"receive!"
3	labhantu	"may they receive"

Principle parts of a few common verbs

Pres ind act	harati "carry"	bhavati "become" / hoti	karoti "make"	gacchati "go"	dadāti "give"	jānāti "know"
" " pass	harīyati		karīyati		dīyati	ñāyati
Imper, 2 sg	hara	bhava, bhavāhi, hohi	karohi	gaccha	dehi	jānāhi
Opt 3 sg	hareyya	bhaveyya, bhave	kare, kareyya	gaccheyya	dadeyya	jāneyya
Fut	harissati	bhavissati	karissati	gamissati	dassati	jānissati
Aor	ahāsi	ahu, bhavi, / ahosi	akāsi	agā, agami, / agamā	adā, adāsi	ajāni, aññāsi
Pres p act	haraṃ	bhavaṃ / bhavanta	karaṃ, karonta	gacchanta	dadaṃ, dadanta	jānaṃ
med	haramāna		kurumāna	gacchamāna	dadamāna / diyamāna (pass)	jānamāna
P p	haṭa	bhūta	kata	gata	datta, dinna	ñāta
F p p	haritabba	bhavitabba	karaṇīya, / katabba, kicca	gamanīya / gantabba	dātabba, deyya	ñeyya, ñātabba
Inf	harituṃ	bhavituṃ	kātuṃ	gantuṃ	dātuṃ	jānituṃ, ñātuṃ
Ger	haritvā	bhavitvā / hutvā	katvā	gamya, gantvā	dātvā	jānitvā, ñatvā

c) Optative

Sg 1	labheyyaṃ, labhe, labheyyāmi	"I should (could, may) receive"
2	labhe, labheyya, labheyyāsi	"you should receive"
3	labhe, labheyya, labheyyāti	"he, she should receive"
Pl 1	labhema, labhemu, labheyyāma	"we should receive"
2	labhetha, labheyyātha	"you should receive"
3	labheyyuṃ, labheyyu	"they should receive"

Note. In 3 sg a medial ending -etha is found.

d) Future tense

Sg 1	labhissāmi	"I will receive"
2	labhissasi	"you will receive"
3	labhissati	"he, she will receive"
Pl 1	labhissāma	"we will receive"
2	labhissatha	"you will receive"
3	labhissanti	"they will receive"

e) Conditional tense (formed from the future stem by adding the prefix a-; endings are the same as in the aorist)

Sg 1	alabhissaṃ	"I were to receive", "I would (have) receive(d)"
2	alabhissa	"you were to receive", "you would (have) receive(d)"
3	alabhissa	"he, she were to receive, would (have) receive(d)"
Pl 1	alabhissāma	"we were to receive, would (have) receive(d)"
2	alabhissatha	"you were to receive, would (have) receive(d)"
3	alabhissaṃsu	"they were to receive, would (have) receive(d)"

f) Aorist tense

We will not give any rules for the formation of the aorist stem, only mention that the augment a- is common, but not necessary. Each aorist will have to be learned as it occurs in the texts. Aorist is nearly always active but there are examples of aorist formed on the passive stem and with passive meaning: vimucci "was freed" (No. 46). Two types of conjugation will here be exemplified.

Sg 1 agamisaṃ, agamiṃ "I went"
2 agami "you went"
3 agami "he, she went"

Pl 1 agamimha "we went"
2 agamittha "you went"
3 agamisuṃ, agamiṃsu "they went"

Sg 1 agamaṃ "I went"
2 agamā "you went"
3 agamā "he, she went"

Pl 1 agamāma, agamamha "we went"
2 agamatha, agamattha "you went"
3 agamuṃ "they went"

g) Some remains of an old perfect tense can be found. Our texts contain just one form: āha, "he said" (No. 1)

h) Pres ind of asmi "I am" is conjugated in this way:

Sg 1 asmi, amhi "I am"
2 asi "you are"
3 atthi "he, she, it is" (can also be used with plural subject)

Pl 1 asmā, amhā "we are"
2 attha "you are"
3 santi "they are"

G 7. Infinite Forms

a) The active present participle is formed by adding the suffix -nt or -nta to the present stem. The medium suffix -māna is also quite common and has active meaning, except when added to the passive stem when the meaning is passive. There is also a suffix -āna. They are inflected as nouns, see G 3a and f.

Examples: gacchant (nom gacchaṃ) "going"
samāna "being"
kayiramāna "being done"

karonta "doing"
sayāna "lying" (No. 36)

b) The past participle usually ends in -ta, sometimes in -na. The meaning is passive, although this rule is not strictly observed. Examples:

gata "gone" (but in No. 36 we must translate: when he goes)
suta "heard"
laddha "received"
vutta "said"
uppanna "produced"
nisinna "seated"
āchanna "covered"
puṭṭha "questioned", but also "having asked"

c) Pali has a future passive participle expressing what should be done or what could be done. It is formed by means of two different suffixes: -tabba and -anīya. Examples:

veditabba "to be known" (No. 1)
pahātabba "to be abandoned" (No. 10)
karanīya "to be done" (No. 18)
labhanīya "attainable" (No. 50)

d) The infinitive ends in -tuṃ or -ituṃ. It is used mainly to express purpose. Its meaning is mainly active but must frequently be translated by passive. Examples:

carituṃ "to move" (No. 26)
gantuṃ "to go"

e) A common way to express subordinated action (corresponding to our temporal and causal clauses) is by using gerundium. It is formed by means of the suffixes -tvā, -tvāna and -ya. The suffix is sometimes difficult to recognize, because of assimilation. Examples:

sutvā "having heard" (No. 26)
pahāya "having left" (No. 26)
pharitvā "having filled" (No. 37)
upasampajja "having attained" (No. 38)
samatikkamma "having passed beyond" (No. 42)
karitvāna "having made" (No. 46)
gahetvāna "having taken" (No. 46)
bandhiya "having bound" (No. 46)

G 8. Compounds

Compounds are not unknown in the English language. They are usually short, like "unknown", "outstanding", "stationmaster", but may reach considerable length, although usually written with hyphen or interspace, like "welfare-reform plan", "river-transport system". They form a special means of grammatical expression: they consist of a series of words, not necessarily nouns, although nouns are most common in English compounds, simply lined up without inflections. The whole unit has a grammatical function in the sentence, as indicated by the inflection of the last component. The Pali compounds fit into the same definition but they are much more varied and may be quite long. We distinguish between the following types:

a) Co-ordinations: aho-rattā (No. 6), "days and nights", soka-parideva-dukkha-domanass-upāyāsā (No. 2) "grief, lamentation, discomfort, unhappiness and despair", assāsa-passāsā (No. 12), "exhalation and inhalation". Here the last member has been given plural form, either because there are several members, each of them singular, or because there are several of each. Alternatively, the neuter singular is used and the compound is treated as a collective noun.

b) Determinative compounds, in which one member stands in some case-relation to the other. The compound may, for instance, be used as a substitute for the genitive or the instrumental case, just as we might say "life-span" instead of "span of life".
Examples: dukkha-samudayo (No. 3), "origin of suffering", kāma-taṇhā (No. 3) "craving for sense-pleasure", satthu-gāravena (No. 1) "out of respect for our teacher", avijjā-anusayo (No. 10) "a tendency to ignorance", sīla-sampanna (No. 18) "endowed with righteousness", kāla-vādin (No. 30) "speaking at the proper time", sammāsambuddha-desita (No. 49) "taught by him who has perfectly understood".

c) Compounds with an adjective as first member:
ariya-sacca (No. 2) "the noble truth", asesa-virāga (No. 4) "complete indifference".

d) Compounds with an adverb as first member:
sammā-sambuddha (No. 49) "one who has completely understood", sammā-diṭṭhi (No. 27) "right view", tatra-abhinandin (No. 3) "finding satisfaction there".

e) Compounds with a conjunction as first member:
yāva-jīvaṃ (No. 32), "as long as they live", yathā-bhūtaṃ (No. 18) "as it really is".

f) Possessive compounds, where a combination of nouns functions as an adjective attribute to something: avijjā-nīvaraṇā sattā (No. 15) "beings with ignorance-obstacle", i e, "beings hindered by ignorance". Note that the compound, although consisting of nouns, is inflected like an adjective and agrees with its head-word; from this we know that it is not independent. In No. 47, sankilesa-dhammo belongs to an implied ahaṃ "I"; its literal meaning is "stain-nature" but it functions here as an adjective and must be translated "having stain-nature", i e "(being) impure by nature". In No. 45 we read ubhato-daṇḍakena ... kakacena, "by means of a two-handled saw" (kakaca, "saw", ubhato "twofold" but literally an abl, daṇḍaka "handle"); here nothing but the context tells us that the compound is possessive. In No. 18 vippaṭisāro is a noun "regret". By adding the negation a- it has been transformed to a possessive compound meaning "free from regret".

Compounds of different types are frequently combined into one unit. Examples: dukkha-nirodha-gāminī-paṭipadā (No. 5) "the suffering--cessation-going-way", i e "the way that goes to the cessation of suffering", surā-meraya-majja-pamāda-ṭhāna (No. 32), where the two first members are coordinated and the others are determinative: "drink-liquor-intoxication-indolence-state", i e, the state of indolence caused by intoxication with drink and liquor". Finally an example from No. 38: viveka-ja-pīti-sukha-sukhuma-sacca-saññā "seclusion-born--joy-happiness-subtle-true-awareness". Here the grammatical relations are varied: pīti and sukha are co-ordinated adjectives; both belong to saññā, the former as object, the latter as attribute. So we translate "a subtle but true awareness of joy and happiness, born of seclusion". A good rule when analyzing long compounds is to start with the last member which generally is the most important one. Long compounds can often be analyzed into two subunits.

All typographical combinations of words are not compounds. Sometimes the combinations just result from the sandhi laws, e g seyyathīdaṃ (No. 5) = seyyathā idaṃ "like this"; nayidha (No. 8) = na idha, "not here"; nāhaṃ (No. 46) = na ahaṃ "not I"; sattūpalabbhati (No. 8) = satto upalabbhati "a person is found". In old Indian writing, the unit was the sentence, not the word; therefore, the words were generally not separated. In European editions, the words are separated, except when the sandhi laws prevent it.

G 9. Pali and Sanskrit

Pali is one of the many dialects which developed from Sanskrit or rather its older Vedic form. The similarities are great. The vocabulary is mainly the same; even words that have no direct equivalents in Sanskrit can generally be derived from roots used in other Sanskrit words. The grammatical means of expression are nearly the same. The differences with regard to sentence construction and syntax are small. There are, however, significant differences with regard to phonetics and inflection. On the whole, these differences are a result of a process of simplification, one mighc say a breaking down and levelling of the older linguistic material. There are fewer sounds in Pali, and a great number of sound combinations have been subjected to assimilations which have reduced the differentiations. The inflectional system has been much simplified and the number of terminations has been reduced, especially with regard to the verbs. At the same time, the great number of alternative forms in Pali shows that the language had not got a definite form: in some cases older inflections have been conserved although a new one had been developed, in other cases declensions or conjugations were mixed up and confused.

Phonetical differences

a) The following examples show how the Pali vowels have developed from Sanskrit (< means "has evolved from")

a < a	Example ajja < adya "today"
< ṛ	kata < kṛta "done"
ā < ā	āsava < āsrava "obsession"
i < i	iti < iti "so"
< ṛ	isi < ṛṣi "sage"
ī < ī	pīti < prīti "joy"
u < u	purisa < puruṣa "man"
< ṛ	uju < ṛju "straight"
< ū	pubba < pūrva "previous"
ū < ū	dūre < dūre "far"
e < e	deva < deva "god"
< ai	veramaṇī < vairamaṇī "abstinence"
o < o	moha < moha "illusion"
< au	yobbana < yauvana "youth"
< as	(in final position only) mano < manas "mind"
< ava	hoti < bhavati "he becomes"

b) Consonants may be single or combined. Most single consonants are the same in Pali as in Sanskrit. An exception is that Pali has just one sibilant, transcribed s, which therefore corresponds to Sanskrit s, ś, ṣ.

s < s sabba < sarva "all"
< ś suñña < śūnya "empty"
< ṣ purisa < puruṣa "man"

Combinations of consonants have generally been assimilated, but sometimes a vowel has been inserted:

arahant < arhant "worthy"
ratana < ratna "jewel"
sineha < sneha "love"
itthī < strī "woman"

Single consonants at the beginning of Pali words sometimes have been produced by assimilation of two:

kh < kṣ khetta < kṣetra "field"
g < gr gīvā < grīvā "neck"
c < ty cāga < tyāga "renunciation"
jh < dhy jhāna < dhyāna "meditation"
ñ < jñ ñāṇa < jñāna "knowledge"
ñ < ny ñāya < nyāya "method"
d < dv dīpa < dvīpa "island"
bh < bhr bhātā < bhrātā "brother"
s < śr suta < śruta "heard"
s < śv sassū < śvaśrū "mother-in-law"
s < sv sagga < svarga "heaven"

Groups of consonants in Pali may have an extremely varied background. We give only a few examples.

kk < kl, ky, kr, kv, tk, rk, lk, kn sukka < śukla "white"
cakka < cakra "wheel"
sakkoti < śaknoti "he can"

kkh < kṣ, kṣṇ, kṣy, khy, tkh, ṣk, ṣkh, sk, skh
bhikkhu < bhikṣu "monk"
sukkha < śuṣka "dry"

gg < gn, gy, gr, gv, dg, rg aggi < agni "fire"
agga < agra "top"
magga < mārga "way"

ggh < ghn, ghy, ghr, dgh, rgh   ugghāta < udghāta "shaking"

cc < cy, ṭy, ty, rc, rty, śc   vuccati < ucyate "it is said"
nicca < nitya "permanent"

cch < kṣ, kṣy, chy, ṭhy, ts, tsy, thy, ps, rch, śch, śy
maccha < matsya "fish"
micchā < mithyā "false"

jj < jy, ḍy, dy, rj   pabbajja < pravrajya "having gone forth"
ajja < adya "today"

jjh < ḍhy, dhy   ajjhatta < adhyātman "subjective"

ññ < jñ, ṇy, ny   viññāṇa < vijñāna "consciousness"
añña < anya "other"

ñh < śn   pañha < praśna "question"

nkh < ṃsk   sankhāra < saṃskāra "activity"

ṇh < kṣṇ, tsn, ṣṇ, sn   taṇhā < tṛṣṇā "thirst"

ṭṭh < ṭhr, ṣṭ, ṣṭr, ṣṭh, sth   aṭṭha < aṣṭau "eight"
tiṭṭhati < tiṣṭhati "he stands"

ḍḍh < ḍhr, rdh   vaḍḍhati < vardhati "he grows"

ṇṇ < ñc, rṇ   vaṇṇa < varṇa "colour"

tt < kt, ktr, tm, tr, tv, pt, rt
ajjhatta < adhyātman "subjective"
rattī < rātrī "night"
cattāro < catvāras "four"
patta < prāpta "obtained"

tth < tr, thr, st, sth, rth   attha < atra "here"
atthi < asti "is"
attha < artha "profit"

dd < dr, dv, bd, rd   bhadda < bhadra "good"
sadda < śabda "sound"

ddh < gdh, dhr, dhv, bdh, rdh   addhan < adhvan "way"
laddha < labdha "received"

pp < tp, py, pr, pv, rp, lp, pn — uppāda < utpāda "appearance"
tappati < tapyate "he is tormented"
sappa < sarpa "snake"
appa < alpa "small"
pappoti < prāpnoti "he obtains"

pph < tph, ṣp, ṣph, sp, sph — puppha < puspa "flower"

bb < db, dv, by, br, rv, lb, lv, vy, vr
nibbāna < nirvāṇa
dibba < divya "divine"
pabbajja < pravrajya "having gone forth"

bbh < dbh, dhv, bhy, bhr, rbh — labbha < labhya "to be taken"
gabbha < garbha "womb"

mm < my, rm — ramma < ramya "pleasant"
kamma < karma "work"

yy < dy, ry — uyyāna < udyāna "park"

ll < ml, rdr, ry, ly, lv — salla < śalya "arrow"

ss < ts, rṣ, rṣy, śy, śr, śv, ṣy, ṣv, sy, sr, sv, rś
vassa < varṣa "rain"
passati < paśyati "he sees"
massu < śmaśru "beard"
assa < aśva "horse"
assa < asya "his"
assa < (a)syāt "he may be"
sahassa < sahasra "thousand"
phassa < sparśa "touch"

Grammatical Differences

As already mentioned the grammar has been very much simplified. The dual number has disappeared from all inflections and has been replaced by the plural. Pali has retained the same nominal stem-forms as Sanskrit but shows a strong preference for vowel stems. Many original consonant stems are treated as vowel stems or have a double form ending in a vowel, generally *-a*. Examples: S *vidyut* "lightning" has developed to *vijju* (*u*-stem), S *tādṛś* "such" to *tādi* (*i*-stem) and *tadin* (*n*-stem). Some *s*-stems have changed either to *-a* or *-sa*, e g S *sumedhas* "wise",

P sumedha (a-stem) or sumedhasa (a-stem). Present participles are either of the old type ending in -nt, or changed to a-stems, e g either bharant "carrying" or bharanta. The case terminations have not been radically changed, the main differences being that genitive and dative are rarely kept apart, while ablative and instrumental plural are always identical and that many of the pronominal terminations are used by the nouns as well. The use of the cases is somewhat less precise and differentiated than in Sanskrit.

As an example, we compare the declension of the a-stems in the two languages: śabda, m "sound".

	Sanskrit	Pali
Nom sg	śabdaḥ	saddo
Voc sg	śabda	sadda
Acc sg	śabdam	saddaṃ
Instr sg	śabdena	saddena (saddā)
Abl sg	śabdāt	saddā (saddasmā, saddamhā, saddato)
Dat sg	śabdāya	saddāya (saddassa)
Gen sg	śabdasya	saddassa
Loc sg	śabde	sadde (saddasmiṃ, saddamhi)
Nom pl	śabdāh	saddā
Voc pl	śabdāh	saddā
Acc pl	śabdān	sadde
Instr pl	śabdaiḥ	saddehi
Abl pl	śabdebhyaḥ	saddehi
Dat pl	śabdebhyah	saddānaṃ
Gen pl	śabdānam	saddānam
Loc pl	śabdeṣu	saddesu

The verbal system has changed more radically.

a) The main tenses in Pali are present, future and aorist. The old imperfect and perfect are retained but have a very restricted use. Imperfect has been incorporated in the aorist and can generally not be distinguished as a separate tense.

b) Sanskrit had a special "medium" conjugation to express reflexive and reciprocal action. This conjugation is also found in Pali but very rarely and without any special meaning. Passive is expressed by means of the same suffix -ya as in Sanskrit but has as a rule active endings.

c) The inflections of the basic tenses are quite similar in cases where few phonetic changes have taken place. To demonstrate this, we compare pres ind and aor of carati "move".

	Sanskrit	Pali
Pres ind		
1. sg	carāmi	carāmi
2. sg	carasi	carasi
3. sg	carati	carati
1. pl	carāmaḥ	carāma
2. pl	caratha	caratha
3. pl	caranti	caranti
Aorist		
1. sg	acāriṣam	acārisaṃ (acariṃ)
2. sg	acārīḥ	acāri
3. sg	acārīt	acāri
1. pl	acāriṣma	acārimha
2. pl	acāriṣṭa	acārittha
3. pl	acāriṣuḥ	acārisuṃ, acariṃsu (acāruṃ)

d) A few parallels will show that many verb forms that look irregular in Pali, can be easily explained in terms of regular phonetic changes:

Pres pass:

vijjati < vidyate "he is found"
haññati < hanyate "he is killed"
dissati < dṛśyate "he is seen"
labbhati < labhyate "he is received"
vuccati < udyate "he is said"
(ni)rujjhati < rudhyate "he is obstructed"

Aorist:

adā < adāt "he gave"
assosi < aśrauṣīt "he heard"
akāsi < akārṣīt "he made"
aññāsi < ajñāsīt "he understood"
addakkhi < adrākṣīt "he saw"

Future tense:

checchati < chetsyati "he will cut"
dakkhiti < drakṣyati "he will see"
sakkhīti < śaksyati "he will be able"

Past participle:

kaṭa < kṛta "done"
vutta < ukta "said"
puṭṭha < pṛṣṭa "asked"
vuddha < vṛddha "grown"
phuṭṭha < spṛṣṭa "touched"
laddha < labdha "received"
diṭṭha < dṛṣṭa "seen"

Future passive participle:

kattabba < kartavya "to be done"

Gerund:

gamma < gamya "having gone"
pecca < pretya "having died"

BIBLIOGRAPHY

Introductions

Buddhadatta Thera, The New Pali Course, Vol. 1-2 (Colombo 4th and 6th ed., 1954-62) A simple introduction with exercises.

- " - The Higher Pali Course for Advanced Students (The Colombo Apothecaries' Co., Ltd, Colombo, 1951). Presents irregular declensions and conjugations but the main part is concerned with syntactical problems.

- " - Aids to Pali Conversation and Translation (Piyaratna, Ambangoda, no date). Gives examples of letters, essays and conversations on varied modern subjects.

Warder, A.K., Introduction to Pali (Pali Text Society, London, 1963). A thorough and pedagogically well-planned book for beginners and not altogether beginners.

Grammars

Geiger, W., Pali: Literature and Language (Univ. of Calcutta, 1943, and Delhi 1968, originally published 1916 in German in "Grundriss der Indo-Arischen Philologie und Altertumskunde"). A full treatment of the phonology and morphology of the language from historical point of view. The section about Pali literature is very brief.

Mayrhofer, Manfred, Handbuch des Pali, Vol. I-II (Carl Winter, Heidelberg, 1951). Written from a comparative point of view. Vol. II contains texts and vocabulary.

Texts

Andersen, D., A Pali Reader, Vol. I-II (Copenhagen and Leipzig, revised ed. 1907-17, Reprint: Kyoto, 1968). Part I contains texts, mainly stories from the Jātaka, and Part II a vocabulary to these texts and, in addition, to the Dhammapada.

Horner, I.B., Ten Jataka Stories (Luzac & Co, Ltd, London, 1957). Contains Pali texts and translation. A convenient book of readings, when the grammar has been mastered, but there is no vocabulary.

Radhakrishnan, S., The Dhammapada, with Introductory Essays, Pali Text, English Translation and Notes (Oxford Univ. Press, London, 1950). A good textbook for students who want to try a more difficult text. There is no vocabulary.

Dictionaries

Buddhadatta Mahāthera, Concise Pāli-English Dictionary (U. Chandradasa de Silva, Colombo 2nd ed. 1968).

- " - English-Pali Dictionary (Pali Text Society, Colombo 1955). Gives equivalents also to modern concepts.

Rhys Davids, T.W. and Stede, W. (Eds.) Pali-English Dictionary (Pali Text Society, London, 1921). A comprehensive and really good dictionary.

History

Barnett, L.D., Antiquities of India (Philip Lee Warner, London, 1913).

Franz, H.G., Buddhistische Kunst Indiens (VEB.A. Seemann, Leipzig, 1965).

Keith, B., Buddhist Philosophy in India and Ceylon (The Clarendon Press, Oxford, 1923).

Lamotte, E., 'Histoire du Bouddhisme Indien des origines à l'ère Śaka (Univ. de Louvain, Bibliothèque du Muséon, Vol. 43, Louvain, 1958).

Malalasekera, G.P. (Ed.), Encyclopaedia of Buddhism (Publ. by the Government of Ceylon, from 1961. Of this comprehensive work, only eight fascicles treating words beginning in A up to Bh had been published in 1971).

Nyanatiloka Thera, Buddhist Dictionary (Frewin & Co Ltd, Colombo, 1950, 2nd ed. 1956).

Radhakrishnan, S., Indian philosophy, Vol. 1 (George Allen & Unwin, London, rev.ed. 1931).

Renou, L., and Filliozat, J., L'Inde Classique (Vol. 1: Payot, Paris, 1947; Vol. 2: Imprimerie Nationale, Paris, 1953).

Thomas, E.J. The Life of Buddha as Legend and History (Routledge and Kegan Paul Ltd, London, 1927).

- " - The History of Buddhist Thought (Routledge and Kegan Paul Ltd, London, 1933).

Warder, A.K. Indian Buddhism (Motilal Banarsidass, Bungalow Rd., Jawahar Nagar, Delhi, 1970).

Winternitz, Moriz, Geschichte der indischen Literatur. Vol. I-III. (K.F. Kochler Verlag, Stuttgart, 1908-1920. Reprint 1968. English translation, "History of Indian Literature" published by Univ. of Calcutta). Vol. II includes Pali literature.

APPENDIX

TWO TYPES OF SECURITY

The following song from Sutta Nipāta is a dialogue between the Buddha and the cowherd Dhaniya. The latter declares that he is rich and has made careful preparations, so he is not afraid of rains. The Buddha replies that he also feels quite secure - but for very different reasons. Suddenly a violent rain comes and Dhaniya sees his security shattered. He and his wife are converted to the Buddha's way of thinking. Then a voice of temptation (Māra) interferes, saying that possessions (here a word with a double meaning) are the delight of man, but is refuted by the Buddha.

This text has a number of not so common forms but is otherwise easy. A vocabulary and a word-for-word translation are provided, but not a complete translation. It is hoped that the reader will be able to make this for himself and will consider it a stimulating test of his ability to understand Pali after completing the book.

Dhaniya-sutta
section

18.	"Pakkodano	duddhakhīro	'ham	asmi",
	(having) boiled rice	(having) drawn milk	I	am
		iti Dhaniyo	gopo	
		so	cowherd	
	"anutīre	Mahiyā	samānavāso;	
	on the bank	of Mahi	with equals living	

Vocabulary and Commentary. sutta, nt, thread, section, text.
18. pakka, ripe, boiled, - odana, m nt boiled rice, - duddha, milked (p p of dohati, milk), - khīra, nt, milk, - The possessive compounds are a way of expressing ownership: "I have rice that is boiled and milk that is drawn", - gopa, m, cowherd, - anutīre (anu, along, tīra, nt, shore), loc as adv, on the bank of, - Mahiyā, gen of Mahi, name of a river, - samāna similar, equal, - vāsa, adj. staying, living, -

channā kuṭi, āhito gini, -
roofed hut having fuel fire

atha ce patthayasī, pavassa deva".
so if you want rain (o) god

19. "Akkodhano vigatakhīlo 'ham asmi",
free from anger (having) the obstructions gone I am

iti Bhagavā,
so the Master

"anutīre Mahiy' ekarattivāso,
on the bank of Mahi one night living

vivaṭā kuṭi, nibbuto gini, -
without roof hut extinguished fire

atha ce patthayasī, pavassa deva."
so if you want rain (o) god

---

channa (p p of chādeti), covered, thatched, - kuṭī, f, hut (also kuṭi, as here; fem nouns on -ī are inflected as nouns on -i, except for nom sg, G 3 c), - āhita (p p of ā - dahati, put), put up, - gini, m, fire, - patthayati, wish (pres 2 sg; -ī for metrical reasons), - pavassati, begin to rain (imper in text), - deva, m, god (voc): "so if you like, o god, let the rain come!" -

19. kodha, m, anger, akkodhana, free from anger, friendly, - vigata, gone away (p p of vigacchati, disappear), - khīla, m, stake, obstacle; or, more probably, poetic form of khila, m, desert, mental obstruction (referring to rāga, dosa, moha, "desire, hate, illusion"), - bhagavant, fortunate, illustrious; commonly used referring to the Buddha, therefore translated "the Master", - eka, one, - ratti, f, night, - vivaṭa, p p, uncovered, open (vivarati, uncover), - nibbuta, p p, extinguished (of fire; the word is etymologically and semantically related to nibbāna; here the meaning is of course double, since "fire" is a common metaphor for passions and desires in Buddhist terminology).

20. "Andhakamakasā na vijjare",
gad-flies (and, G 8a) mosquitoes not are found

iti Dhaniyo gopo

"kacche rūḷhatiṇe caranti gāvo,
in pasture (with) grown grass roam cows

vutthim pi saheyyuṃ āgatam, -
rain even they should endure (if) come

atha ce patthayasī, pavassa deva."

21. "Baddhā hi bhisī susankhatā", iti Bhagavā,
bound for raft well constructed

"tinno pāragato vineyya ogham
having crossed gone beyond would leave flood

attho bhisiyā na vijjati, -
use of raft not is found

atha ce patthayasī, pavassa deva."

---

20. *andhaka*, m, "blind fly", gad-fly,- *makasa*, m, mosquito, - *vindati*, find; pass *vijjati*: the form here is 3 pl med, G 6, - *kaccha*, nt, long grass, grass-field (loc), - *rūḷha*, p p, grown (*rūhati*, grow), - *tiṇa*, nt, grass, - *carati*, move about, - *go*, m & f, cow; it is inflected as follows:

	sg		pl
nom	go	nom	gāvo
acc	gavaṃ, gāvam	acc	gāvo
instr	gavena, gāvena	instr	gohi
dat, gen	gavassa	dat, gen	gonaṃ, gavaṃ, gunnaṃ
abl	gavamhā, gavā	abl	gohi
loc	gavamhi, gāvimhi, gave	loc	gosu, gavesu

vuṭṭhi, f, rain, - *sahati*, endure (3 pl opt), - *āgata*, p p, come (*ā-gacchati*).

21. *baddha*, p p, bound together, built (*bandhati*, bind), - *bhisi*, f, raft (-*ī* in the text is perhaps the original ending), - *sankhata*, p p, constructed (*sankharoti*, put together), - *tiṇṇa*, p p, (having) crossed, overcome (*tarati*, pass over), - *pāragata*, p p, (having) gone beyond, - *vineti*, remove, leave (3 sg opt), - *ogha*, m, flood, -*attha*, m, interest, use.

22.	"Gopī	mama	assavā	alolā",	iti Dhaniyo gopo,
	wife	my	obedient	modest	

"dīgharattaṃ	saṃvāsiyā	manāpā,
a long time	living with (me)	lovely

tassā	na	suṇāmi	kiñci	pāpaṃ, -
(gen) of her	not	I hear	anything	bad

atha ce patthayasī, pavassa deva."

23.	"Cittaṃ	mama	assavaṃ	vimuttaṃ",	iti Bhagavā,
	mind	my	obedient	liberated	

"dīgharattaṃ	paribhāvitaṃ	sudantaṃ,
a long time	developed	well tamed

pāpam	pana	me	na	vijjati, -
bad	then	in me	not	is found

atha ce patthayasī, pavassa deva."

24.	"Attavetanabhato	'ham	asmi",	iti Dhaniyo gopo,
	self earning supported	I	am	

"puttā	ca	me	samāniyā	arogā,
sons	and	my	together	not ill

tesaṃ	na	suṇāmi	kiñci	pāpam,
of them	not	I hear	anything	bad

atha ce patthayasī, pavassa deva."

---

22. *gopī*, f, cowherdess (f to *gopa*), wife of cowherd, - *assava*, obedient, - *alola*, not greedy, modest, - *dīgha*, long, - *ratta*, nt, night, time, - *saṃvāsiya*, living together with, - *manāpa*, charming ("for a long time the lovely one has been living with me; I never hear anything bad about her"), - *suṇāti*, hear, - *kiñci*, indefinite pron, n, anything (m: *koci*, f: *kāci*), - *pāpa*, evil, bad.

23. *vimutta*, p p, liberated, free (*vimuñcati*, release), - *paribhāvita*, p p, trained, developed (*paribhāveti*, build up), - *danta*, p p, tamed (*dameti*, domesticate).

24. *vetana*, nt, earning, - *bhata*, supported, - *samāna*, equal, here instr f, equally, together, - *roga*, m, illness ("my sons are healthy and live with me").

25. "Nāhaṃ bhatako 'smi kassaci", iti Bhagavā,
not I servant am of anybody (gen of koci).

"nibbiṭṭhena carāmi sabbaloke,
with (my pay) received I walk around in all the world

attho bhatiyā na vijjati, -
use of fee not is found

atha ce patthayasī, pavassa deva."

26. "Atthi vasā, atthi dhenupā", iti Dhaniyo gopo,
is (are) cows is (are) suckling calves

"godharaṇiyo paveṇiyo pi atthi,
ready to breed heifers even is (are)

usabho pi gavampatī ca atthi, -
bull even lord of cows and is

atha ce patthayasī, pavassa deva."

27. "N'atthi vasā, n'atthi dhenupā," iti Bhagavā,
not is (are) cows not is (are) suckling calves

"godharaṇiyo paveṇiyo pi n'atthi,
ready to breed heifers even not is (are)

usabho pi gavampatīdha n'atthi, -
bull even lord of cows here not is

atha ce patthayasī, pavassa deva."

---

25. bhataka, m, servant, lit "a man who is fed", - *nibbiṭṭha*, p p of *nibbisati*, receive (one's pay when a work is completed: "I walk around in all the world with my task done", i e "completely free") - *bhati*, f, fee, lit "support". The words *bhata*, *bhataka* and *bhati* are related etymologically, and we have here a play on the literal meanings. Dhaniya has admitted that he is *bhata*, "supported" and therefore "dependent". The Buddha denies that he is dependent on anything.

26. *vasā*, f, cow, - *dhenupa*, m, suckling calf, - *godharaṇī*, adj f, ready to breed, - *paveṇi*, f, succession, here concrete: offspring, heifer, - *usabha*, m, bull, - *gavampati*, m, lord of cows (-*ī* for metric reasons; "and there is even a bull, the lord of cows").

27. *idha*, adv, here.

28. "Khīlā nikhātā asampavedhī", iti Dhaniyo gopo,
posts dug in unmovable

"dāmā muñjamayā navā susaṇṭhānā,
cords made of rush new well formed

na hi sakkhinti dhenupā pi chettuṃ, -
not for shall be able calves even to break

atha ce patthayasī, pavassa deva."

29. "Usabho-r- iva chetvā bandhanāni", iti Bhagavā,
bull as having broken (G 7 e) fetters

"nāgo pūtilataṃ va dālayitvā,
elephant stinking creeper as having broken

nāhaṃ puna upessaṃ gabbhaseyyaṃ, -
not I again shall enter womb-bed

atha ce patthayasī, pavassa deva."

30. Ninnañ ca thalañ ca pūrayanto
low and high flooding

mahāmegho pāvassi tāvad eva.
great cloud started to rain just then

---

28. khīla, m, stake, post, - nikhāta, p p, dug in, driven in (nikhanati, dig into), - sampavedhin, to be shaken (sam-pa-vedhati, tremble violently), - dāma, nt, rope, cord, - muñja, m, a sort of grass, rush (Saccharum munja), - -maya, made of, - nava, new, - saṇṭhāna, nt, form, - sakkoti, be able (fut sakkhati, 3 pl sakkhinti), - chindati, cut off, break (inf: chettuṃ; gerundium, v 29: chetvā).

29. usabho-r-iva: r is an inserted sandhi vowel (but is in reality historically justified), - bandhana, nt, fetter, - nāga, m,elephant,- pūti-latā, f, "stinking creeper", a sort of creeper, Cocculus cordifolius (pūti, rotten, latā, f, creeper), - dalati, burst, caus dāleti, break up, here gerundium, G 7 e, - upeti, go to, enter (here fut 1 sg, upessaṃ; the ending -aṃ can be used instead of -āmi), - gabbha-seyyā, f, womb (gabbha, m, womb, seyyā, f, bed),- Translate: "Like a bull who has broken his fetters and like an elephant who has burst a creeper I shall not again enter a womb (i e, be reborn)".

30. ninna, low, - thala, high, firm, - pūreti, fill, flood (pres p nom sg), - megha, m, cloud, - pavassati, "rain forth", begin to rain (pāvassi is 3 sg aor), - tāva, so much, tāva-d-eva, just then, at once,

Sutvā	devassa	vassato
having heard	the god	raining

imaṃ	atthaṃ	Dhaniyo	abhāsatha:
this	thing		said

31.

"Lābhā	vata	no	anappakā,
to luck	certainly	for us (gen)	not small

ye	mayaṃ	Bhagavantaṃ	addasāma.
who	we	the Master	have seen

Saraṇaṃ	taṃ	upema,	cakkhuma,
(as) refuge	to you (G 4 b)	we go	o clear-sighted one

satthā	no	hohi	tuvaṃ	mahāmuni.
teacher	our	become	you	o great sage

32.

Gopī	ca	ahañ	ca	assavā,
wife	and	I		(are) obedient

brahmacariyaṃ	Sugate	carāmase,
the chaste life	with the Happy One	may we live

---

sutvā, gerundium of *suṇāti*, hear, - *vassati*, rain (pres p gen sg; this is a case of "absolute genitive", a construction of a noun followed by a participle, both in the gen: "having heard the god raining", "having heard how the god rained"; the absolute gen is usually translated by a subordinate clause; cf the absolute loc, G 2 g), - *attha*, m, nt, meaning, thing, - *bhāsati*, speak (here 3 sg aor med; more common is aor act *abhāsi*).

31. *lābha*, m, gain (*lābhā*, irregular dat sg, "to gain for somebody"),- *appaka*, small, - *dassati*, see (here 1 pl aor; 1 sg is *addasaṃ*): "It is certainly of no small gain to us that we have seen the Master", - *saraṇa*, nt, shelter, refuge, - *cakkhumant*, having eyes clear-sighted (here voc), - *satthar*, m, teacher, - *hohi*, imper of *bhavati*, become, - *muni*, m, sage.

32. *brahmacariya*, nt, chaste life, - *sugata*, "well gone", happy (frequent epithet of the Buddha), - *carati*, move about (here imper med 1 pl, "may we walk"; with acc: undertake, set out for),

jātimaraṇassa	pāragā	
of birth (and) death	rising above	

dukkhass'	antakarā	bhavāmase."
of suffering	making an end	may we become (imper med 1 pl)

33.

"Nandati	puttehi	puttimā,"	iti	Māro	pāpimā,
rejoices	in sons	owner of sons	so	Māra	evil

"gomiko	gohi	tath'eva	nandati,
owner of cows	in cows	likewise	rejoices

upadhī	hi	narassa	nandanā,
possessions	for	man's	delight

na	hi	so	nandati	yo	nirūpadhi."
not	for	he	rejoices	who	without possessions

34.

"Socati	puttehi	puttimā",	iti Bhagavā,
worries	about sons	having sons	

"gomiko	gohi	tath'eva	socati,
owner of cows	about cows	likewise	worries

upadhī	hi	narassa	socanā,
possessions	for	man's	worry

na	hi	so	socati	yo	nirūpadhī"	ti.
not	for	he	worries	who	without possessions	so

-pāraga, going beyond, - antakara, putting an end to (with gen) (anta, m, end; kara, making).

33. nandati, find delight in (with instr), - puttimant, having sons (putta, m, son), - Māra, m, the god of temptation and death, - pāpimant, evil, - gomika, m, owner of cows, - tath'eva, just so, in the same way, - upadhi, m, possession (as object of desire, and therefore also:) foundation (the word is frequently used as a doctrinal term referring to the karmic effects collected during a persons life and forming the basis of rebirth; here the meaning is concrete, but in v 34 both meanings are intended), - nandanā, f, delight.

34, socati, grieve,worry_about, - socanā, f, sorrow, worry, - nirūpadhi, free from possessions.

www.ingramcontent.com/pod-product-compliance
Ingram Content Group UK Ltd.
Pitfield, Milton Keynes, MK11 3LW, UK
UKHW020349010325
455677UK00021B/363